TYPOGRAPHIC YEARS

TYPOGRAPHIC YEARS

A PRINTER'S JOURNEY THROUGH

A HALF CENTURY

1925 – 1975

BY JOSEPH BLUMENTHAL

FREDERIC C. BEIL · NEW YORK

ACKNOWLEDGMENTS

THE PRACTICE of a craft during a long, turbulent, and creative period has involved the hearts and minds of many men and women. Among them are the writers and artists whose talents give substance and form to the book, the men who set the type and print the sheets, the makers of paper, the binders of books, and, not least, the institutions and collectors at whose call the printing is produced. To all my co-workers who have played their parts in our typographic adventure, this volume is dedicated with profound respect and affection.

The persuasion that led to the writing of these pages came several years ago from Horace Hart, who also spoke for the Grolier Club's Committee on Publications. The manuscript has had the good fortune of concern by scholars and practitioners in our small world of fine printing, to whom I am deeply in debt for invaluable comments and corrections. The whole text was read by Howard I. Gralla, Abe Lerner, and Horace Hart. Pertinent sections were read by John Dreyfus, Charles Ryskamp, Frederick B. Adams, Donald S. Klopfer, Bradford D. Kelleher, H. George Fletcher, Jerry Kelly, Herbert H. Johnson, and others.

The Grolier Club, in publishing a limited edition for its members, has again proved its long-standing commitment to the arts of the book. Elizabeth M. Riley, Chairman of the Committee on Publications, Robert Nikirk, the Club's Librarian, Leonard Schlosser and Frederic C. Beil, members of the Club's Council, have contributed their wisdom and dedication. C. Freeman Keith at The Stinehour Press and John F. Peckham at The Meriden Gravure Company have printed type and illustrations with their usual devotion. To all who have shared in making this book a reality I offer humble thanks. And that, of course, includes my wife, inseparable part of a memorable half century.

J. B.

THE
TABLE
OF
CONTENTS

TYPOGRAPHIC YEARS *page* 3

BEGINNINGS 7

THE SPIRAL PRESS 17

EARLY YEARS 19

THE NINETEEN TWENTIES 25

WHY PRINTING? 28

SEPARATION OF PRINTER AND DESIGNER 29

THE AMERICAN INSTITUTE OF GRAPHIC ARTS 31

GERMANY AND HOLLAND 34

ROBERT FROST AT THE SPIRAL PRESS 37

THE COLOPHON 43

THE DEPRESSION 46

OF TYPE AND THE ALPHABET 47

EMERSON TYPE 53

PRINTING ON THE HAND PRESS 60

THE LIMITED EDITIONS CLUB 66

WHAT MAKES FINE PRINTING FINE 71

PRINTING EDUCATION 74

THE MUSEUM OF MODERN ART 82

THE PUBLIC PAPERS AND ADDRESSES OF
    FRANKLIN D. ROOSEVELT 84

THE TYPOPHILES 86

THE
TABLE
OF
CONTENTS
CONTINUED

PRINTER AS PUBLISHER 89

PRINTING HOUSES AND THE ARTISTS 93

WORLD WAR II 103

THE METROPOLITAN MUSEUM OF ART AND
THE MUSEUM PRESS 106

STEUBEN GLASS 109

INSTITUTIONS AND FOUNDATIONS 111

THE GROLIER CLUB 116

THE PIERPONT MORGAN LIBRARY 118

LIQUIDATION AND DISPERSAL 126

ART OF THE PRINTED BOOK 127

THE PRINTED BOOK IN AMERICA 131

THE HEROIC GENERATION 137

EXHIBITIONS 140

TYPOGRAPHIC YEARS

TYPOGRAPHIC
YEARS

A printer's journey through a half century

THIS BOOK is a printer's journey through the half century that followed one world war and survived another: a passage through fifty years that sustained a major depression, produced a technological revolution, and witnessed vast changes in society.

The 1920's was an affluent and expansive decade that produced great men and women and great events. In the art of the printed book it was a summit of heroic achievement in America and in Europe. The beginnings of a renaissance in printing can be seen in the procession of noble books that came from the Kelmscott Press of William Morris in England during the 1890's and during the same decade in the United States when a remarkable confluence of typographic genius appeared in New England. In 1891, when Morris completed his first Kelmscott book, *The Story of the Glittering Plain*, Thomas B. Mosher in Portland, Maine, published George Meredith's *Modern Love*, the first of Mosher's long list of attractively designed small books of impeccable literary taste. The next forty years would witness the production of many beautiful books. Volumes were printed and published that compare favorably with the best work produced during the five centuries since the appearance of Gutenberg's great legacy to mankind. A number of private presses in England and on the Continent, following the

3

Kelmscott example, achieved volumes of true grandeur. In the United States conditions were favorable for the work of Bruce Rogers, Daniel Berkeley Updike, Frederic W. Goudy, and others during four resplendent decades. Then came the Great Depression of 1929.

The ravages of the Depression that lasted into the middle and late thirties, and the leveling of privileged wealth that followed, brought to an end the production of magnificent press books that had enshrined man's finest poetry and prose in monumental pages of paper and type. Nevertheless, during the twenties and thirties, a number of new, small printing houses were set up in several parts of the country by competent and idealistic young men who would be faithful to the best traditions of their craft. Fortunately, they survived the Depression.

Inasmuch as the words "fine printing" (inaccurate and insufficient in themselves) will appear throughout these pages, perhaps a clarifying paragraph from my preface to *The Printed Book in America* (1977) should be repeated here: "Fine printing involves an esthetic dedication. It is an expression of the human spirit which, through the arrangement and presentation of the printed word, reaches toward order and harmony and beauty. Fine printing implies scholarship, artistry, and craftsmanship at the command of the practitioner, whether in printing houses, at private presses, or in workshops of college art departments — whether on automatic machinery or on hand equipment."

Printing houses have been the citadel of fine printing in the United States since the 1890's, when Daniel Berkeley Updike established the Merrymount Press in Boston. "Printing house" is the proper designation, I believe, for a relatively small, scholarly printing establishment where high and rather inflexible standards of design and execution are maintained by the owner-director of the press. What set the printing house apart from the average commercial printer was scholarship and an articulated sense of craft.

4

The private press, on the other hand, which cannot be described within exact limits, normally has been the serious pursuit of a learned person of independent means, or the avocational interest of an able practitioner in a related area such as the faculty of a college art department. (The productive private press should not be confused with the hobbyist happily setting type on a Sunday afternoon.) Books issued in the private press tradition are chosen solely at the pleasure of the persons involved. Most of the printers discussed later in these pages would occasionally indulge their desire to make volumes of their own choice on which they could lavish their own time and equipment. For some of these printers their publications became a vital activity and source of income. Distribution has always been a responsibility of a private press, inasmuch as books once completed must be brought to market. A surprisingly large number of private presses are now active because members of a new generation, in rebellion against massive industrialism, have turned to the dignity and fulfillment of hand labor. Much of the work is excellent. Accepting and enjoying its limitations, they are setting type by hand and printing on hand presses.

The printing houses with which the present volume is primarily concerned were letterpress printers. Letterpress is that ancient and forthright method whereby inked metal type is impressed directly on and into paper. Properly done, the process involves incised depth, however slight. But depth is that wonderful and subtle achievement that escapes the quick awareness in printing as it does in other areas of the human condition. Although Linotype machines and huge modern presses developed great speed, the direct impression of type on paper remained fundamental until the middle years of the present century when electronic "type" composition photographed on film spelled the end of metal type in the marketplace, and the spread of printing by offset rendered letterpress all but obsolete.

5

Updike's Merrymount Press in Boston and the Printing House of William Edwin Rudge in Mount Vernon just outside New York City—each with some thirty-five employees, composing machines, and cylinder presses—were the largest fine presses in the United States during the first half of this century. With their high standards of design and production, both shops became exemplars for the handful of young men who set up their own presses, east and west. These young men combined scholarship and craftsmanship with business acumen—a rare combination. They were not professional artists, i.e., neither painters nor printmakers. But as designers and printers they had creative talent capable of delivering significant books and ephemera within economic realities. With few exceptions, they were dependent for livelihood on the printing they produced in their shops. They became thoroughgoing professionals at their work. In addition to the collectors who bought press books, patronage for significant printing came from cultural institutions, such as museums, libraries, universities, foundations, special publishers and booksellers, art galleries, book clubs, and those rare individuals for whom the printed page touched special chords.

The small but well-equipped printing houses enjoyed a secondary purpose of prime importance. They provided hospitable space and working conditions for professional artists and designers whose cultural inclinations led them to the printed page that they honored and embellished. From the artist-printer alliances thus formed —a phenomenon of the period—came a resurgence of type design, high-spirited promotional printing, and notable illustrated books.

Whether small, scholarly printing houses will survive in an increasingly mechanistic world, or what will take their place, cannot be foreseen. Change, as we know, has been inherent since the invention of the wheel. In recent times society has survived the transition from sail to steam, and from steam to electricity. Now we must adjust to a computerized world. Those persons who may be apprehensive of change should remember that the introduction of

6

printing from movable type in the fifteenth century made the magnificent Medieval and Renaissance manuscript obsolete, including its scribes and illuminators. But the new invention brought with it a priceless potential—the spread of learning to the whole of society. And in due course the art of the book replaced the more effulgent art of the manuscript. May we not expect for the future what has happened in the past—that human ingenuity and aspiration, with its urge for knowledge and beauty, will again turn social and technological change to society's advantage?

The Spiral Press, which I established in 1926, fulfills, I believe, the conditions defined above for a small printing house engaged in fine printing. It is my ardent wish that my fifty years as a typographic designer and printer will serve as a microcosm whereby the typographic currents and events of a remarkable half century may be seen in their historical setting. In the pages that follow, I will first give some personal background and then enlarge.

BEGINNINGS

The exodus of immigrants from Europe to America during the second half of the nineteenth century included ambitious and adventurous young lads who looked to the new land for opportunities they could not find at home. My forebears were among them. My maternal grandfather came from Germany, arrived in Indiana shortly before the Civil War, and fought for the Union. My father left Germany at fourteen years of age and arrived in the United States in the early 1870's to seek the immigrant's good fortune. Relatives who had preceded him to Altoona, Pennsylvania, lent him the few dollars needed to equip him with needles and pins, ribbons and thread, and other household articles that he put in the pack on his back. He walked from farm to farm in central Pennsylvania, where lonely housewives welcomed these pink-cheeked youngsters from the far world, purchased their wares, and let them sleep in the barn. After a few years, the adroit lad was able to buy a horse and buggy and carried enough merchandise to acquire the status of a traveling salesman. Next followed enough savings to buy a store in the town and to rise to the respectability of an American merchant. The promised land kept its promise to the former peddler who later moved to the larger world of New York and sent his three children to American colleges—another American dream fulfilled.

I was born in New York in 1897 and moved through the normal twelve years of city public schools, then went to Cornell University as a member of the class of 1919. When the United States entered World War I in 1917, a feeling of patriotic duty existed among the young, a patriotism that was soon crushed by the cynicism that followed the inhuman mass slaughter of trench warfare. In the spring of 1917, when President Woodrow Wilson asked the Congress to declare war on Germany, I joined that half of my sophomore class that left for home and enlistment. I was accepted by the glamorous Naval Aviation unit with its sky-blue uniform and golden wings. But the only wound stripes I received during the next two years were for appendicitis and related casualties. The war was won although I never went aloft to drop a bomb, much to my chagrin in 1918, but to my later profound gratitude.

It had been my father's wish that I would carry on in business where he had left off, that I should rise to be a captain of industry. Alas, I never became more than a corporal. Despite a running start that included selling trips to South America, the West Indies, and Mexico in the early 1920's, I decided at age twenty-six that strictly business was not enough to fill my life. Books and reading, thanks primarily to my mother, had been a commonplace in our home, and I came to the conviction that I would prefer to earn my livelihood somewhere in the world of the book. So, in 1924 I wrote a letter to every publisher in New York asking for a job. The only reply, except for perfunctory letters of refusal, came from Mr. B. W.

Huebsch, who invited me to come in for a bit of "helpful talk." Huebsch was a small publisher of vision and courage who issued the early work of Sherwood Anderson, Theodore Dreiser, James Joyce, and other writers, some of whom were considered controversial or immoral, or both. Furthermore, he took special interest in the physical appearance of his books. This was the period when noteworthy cultivated individuals owned and directed their own publishing houses, and when knowledgeable booksellers conducted their own personal bookshops. By good fortune the friendly chat soon turned into a job. My duties as a Huebsch assistant included a sales trip through the Middle West and South. Travel then was by train, much of it in overnight sleeping cars. However, it was on a selling mission in a New York bookshop that I came upon the early volumes of the Nonesuch Press and heard such names as Bruce Rogers and Daniel Berkeley Updike.

The Nonesuch Press had issued its first book, John Donne's *Love Poems*, in 1923. It was a handsome, tall, and slender octavo, set in the Fell types, printed at the Oxford University Press on a splendid French handmade paper, bound in quarter vellum with decorated Italian paper sides. It was the first press book I had ever seen, and it made a strong impression on me. I bought a copy for five dollars and took special pleasure in the paper, the arrangement of type, the binding, and the whole feel of the book. It was a new and deeply felt experience.

After I had been with Mr. Huebsch for only a half year, he found that the economics of a rapidly expanding society made the existence of a small, independent publishing house extremely difficult. He joined forces with Harold K. Guinzburg at the then new Viking Press to their great mutual benefit. This was the middle twenties, when a host of young Americans became a "generation in exile" in Paris. Aware that I had not completed my education, I decided to spend the next year in Europe in reading and travel and, hopefully, in some personal growth. It was then (1925/26)

9

possible to take ship to Europe in nondeluxe accommodations, stay a modest year, and return—all on one thousand American dollars. My shipmates were a merry group of young writers, artists, and academicians from many parts of the country, all intent on finding personal expansion and wider horizons in the ancient cities of an older civilization. Most of these young people went first to Paris, where they knew that Gertrude Stein, Ernest Hemingway, James Joyce, and other expatriates might be seen in some boulevard café. It was the time when Joyce's *Ulysses* could be bought at Sylvia Beach's Shakespeare and Company bookshop and smuggled through customs on return to the United States. *Ulysses* was later published in the United States by Random House, thanks to a landmark decision in 1933 by Judge John Munro Woolsey that marked the beginning of a period of greater tolerance. The book, designed by Ernst Reichl for Random House, was an early and courageous attempt to introduce modern design into traditional book production.

I went first to London, where I found the bookish city I had hoped to find. Charing Cross Road was then lined with bookstalls where one might purchase the classics of literature in pleasant, old, and inexpensive editions. Thus I spent my days reading, often on a bench in one of London's many lovely parks in good weather, or when it rained, in my furnished room on Gower Street near the British Museum. Long hours were passed happily in that noble institution where I began to feel a strong pull toward the handsomely printed books on exhibition.

The English private-press movement, sparked by William Morris, which had produced such glories as the Doves Press Bible and the Ashendene Dante on hand presses, had taken a turn toward the use of the machine in the twenties, primarily because of the genius of Francis Meynell of the Nonesuch Press. Scion of a distinguished English literary and publishing family, Meynell had spent several years as a printer in the design of books and advertising matter. He established the Nonesuch Press in 1923. The stated purpose of the

Press was "to choose and make books according to a triple ideal: significance of subject, beauty of format, and moderation of price." These commendable objectives were achieved in a dramatic thirteen-year program. The books, always handsomely designed by Meynell and printed under his close supervision, were produced by machine in several British plants, including the printing houses of Oxford and Cambridge universities.

Two men—Bruce Rogers, American, and Francis Meynell, English—were responsible for crossing the abyss between the grandeur of books produced in the hand tradition of the private press to noble books designed and printed by devoted professionals in control of power-driven machinery. Meynell was aware of the books Bruce Rogers had made at the Riverside Press between 1900 and 1912, and looked upon Rogers as his typographic "hero." The procession of Meynell's great books has been celebrated in an illustrated bibliography, *The Nonesuch Century*, published by the Nonesuch Press in 1936, and in *History of the Nonesuch Press* (1981) by John Dreyfus with a descriptive catalogue of all Nonesuch publications.

Among other British private presses active during the twenties, the most noteworthy were the Golden Cockerel Press, which under the guiding hands of Robert Gibbings printed a number of beautiful books; and the Gregynog Press in Wales. Eric Gill (1882–1940), the eminent sculptor and wood engraver, illustrated a number of superb volumes. Especially noteworthy is his magnificent *Four Gospels*, published in 1931. He designed the famous Perpetua type for the Monotype Corporation in London, and set up his own private press for which he cut a proprietary typeface, Joanna.

From London I went to France, Italy, Austria, Germany, and Holland. In each of the chief cities I drifted intuitively to the great repositories of the printed book, notably the Bibliothèque Nationale in Paris, the Biblioteca Laurenziana in Florence, and the Vatican Library in Rome. I hovered over cases of illuminated manuscripts and the noble folios of the early printers. An attachment and direction was being awakened, and I determined to take part, somehow, in the production of books.

On my return to New York I tried to find a job in book production with a publishing house. But eagerness was not enough. Some technical training was essential. Fortunately, at that time, William Edwin Rudge in his fine shop was wonderfully generous to a dozen or more serious young men who believed in good printing as a permanent career. He gave them jobs where they could learn. Later known as the Rudge alumni, the Rudge "graduates" spread out into printing and publishing, where they carried with them the ideals and devotion to workmanship they had found at Mount Vernon.

The Printing House of William Edwin Rudge was a printing house in the best sense. Rudge had started as a boy in his father's small printing shop in downtown New York about 1890, when type in most shops was still being set by hand and small presses were foot-operated. The Linotype machine had been invented and first put to use in the 1880's, but it was some years before the smaller plants adopted machine composition. The young Rudge continued his education at night, including a three-year engineering course at Cooper Union. The Rudge business grew with a rapidly expanding American economy. In 1920 the plant was moved to a handsome, low stone building in Mount Vernon. Although Rudge was not a professional designer nor an academic scholar, he was a great printer. He had an innate sense for quality, with enormous pride and competence in his calling.

When Mr. Rudge hired me, he told me to report to the foreman of the composing room where I would be allowed to learn the trade. By an oversight he failed to so notify the foreman, who took umbrage and refused to acknowledge my existence. The injured gentleman, a Prussian by birth and by accent, made it so difficult for me that I left in a few months. (It so happened that a few years later he applied at the Spiral Press for a job. He did not recognize his former apprentice, neither did I remind him. But for good and sufficient reasons he was not hired.) Nevertheless, at the Rudge plant I was able, thanks to several compassionate compositors, to become familiar with some of the basic aspects of printing. I became aware of the dedication to craftsmanship of Mr. Rudge and the workers in the shop. One of the compositors, James Hendrickson, was especially kind and helpful. He was a Shakespearean actor who became an excellent typographic designer. Had one been able then to look into the future one would have foreseen a lifetime's friendship, with Jim during his last years occupying his desk at the Spiral Press.

Bruce Rogers was working on some of his handsome books that were being produced at the Rudge plant during my months there. Although I did not meet Rogers until several years later, I have always boasted that in my first job in printing I worked directly under the world's greatest book designer. His studio was on the second floor. The composing room, where I was stationed, was on the first floor immediately below him.

There followed a few months at the Marchbanks Press. Hal Marchbanks, bluff and hearty, had come from Texas and in 1914 established his press in New York with capacity to turn out work for concerned publishers and several industrial accounts. His equipment consisted of two large cylinder presses and several smaller automatics. He was an excellent printer; a sound, if conservative, designer addicted to Caslon type; and a faithful member of the graphic group at the National Arts Club. He made his press into a meeting place and hospitable workshop for typographic designers and graphic artists who were at liberty to supervise their own work in production.

Several books were printed for the Limited Editions Club—some designed by the Marchbanks house designer, Edward Alonzo Miller; others from the hands of typographers and illustrators chosen by the publisher, George Macy. Frederic W. Goudy, T. M. Clel-

13

and, and other artists and designers came and went. It was a great thrill for an eager neophyte to see these prominent men at work in a congenial printing house atmosphere. One of the frequent visitors was Thomas N. Fairbanks, the paper merchant who imported handmade and mouldmade papers from most of the great mills of Europe and Asia and stocked them in New York. During the twenties a wide assortment of magnificent papers was made overseas at prices that made their use possible for special books and printed ephemera.

I begged Mr. Marchbanks for a job, not knowing then that eager and ambitious college boys were more of a burden than a help in a busy shop. Nevertheless, Marchbanks was patient with me, if rather reluctant, and told me to report to the superintendent of the plant. In answer to my (unwarranted) question about wages, Marchbanks said he would pay me whatever I was worth. He kept his promise—at the end of the week he paid me nothing.

At the end of the first day, George Hoffman, the plant superintendent, intending to fire me, called me to his desk and asked me how I could possibly hope to hold a job there without experience or competence. I suggested that he come to my apartment and have a cup of coffee because I couldn't answer in a word. He consented, and we bought sandwiches on the way to my one-room apartment in Greenwich Village. As we talked, it became clear that Hoffman, who had left Germany a few years earlier, was thoroughly conversant with the new and vital era of printing in that country and had been acquainted with many of its leading type designers and printers. Printing in Germany had reached a high level in several excellent plants. A number of publishers turned out books distinguished in design and production. There were also several exceptional private presses, most important being the Cranach and Bremer presses. Art and craft schools flourished, and a number of graphic artists turned to typography. These men, among others, were responsible for very interesting new type designs. Later, Hoffman and I would buy several of these faces before they were imported and sold in the United States by the Continental Type Founders.

After several cups of coffee, and talking late into the night, Hoffman and I decided, in our innocence, to set up an after-hours private press. The start was made with a foot-operated 12 x 18 inch Golding job press. Next came the search for a suitable small book to print and eventually publish. I was not interested in turning out still another *Sonnets from the Portuguese* or a *Rubáiyát of Omar Khayyám*. I wanted to do something of contemporary interest.

Through a New York art dealer, J. B. Neumann, I learned that Max Weber, one of America's leading modern artists (whose work was part of the famous Armory Show of avant-garde art in 1913), had written some poems and had cut illustrative woodcuts to go with the verse. I called on Weber, then no longer a young man, at his home in Great Neck, Long Island. I was thrilled by the blocks, if less so by the poetry, but much pleased by the unity of the work and its suitability for a small, special publication. Weber responded with enthusiasm to the prospect of having his poems set by hand and printed on handmade paper, and of seeing the blocks in a book made with loving care. The little blocks were all 2 x 4¼ inches and about ⅛ inch thick. A friend had given Weber a gift of some honey, and these pieces of wood were from the boxes in which comb honey was then sold.

Weber used his penknife on these fragments of wood and made them into little compositions of great beauty, cutting for depth and scraping for texture much in the manner of Gauguin. He offered to pull some proofs for me then and there. "Do you have a press?" I asked. "No, but I will print some for you." He touched appropriate parts of each block with oil paint—a different color on each fingertip—put the block and a piece of Japanese paper on the floor, set a telephone book on top of that, and then, short and rotund, stood on the book. Out came a beautiful color print—really a monotype, since each print would be of somewhat different colors. I looked with wonder and awe at the power of printing that could evoke and produce beauty from such simple materials and tools. As an incipient printer and publisher I was profoundly pleased at the potentials in my proposed profession.

The poems and blocks printed on our Golding job press, two pages at a time, finally materialized into a book in October 1926—our incunable. Entitled *Primitives*, the edition was 350 copies, the price $7.50 per copy. The type I chose was called "Pen Print Bold," available for hand composition from the American Type Founders Company. It was a rugged, rather primitive design that, I felt, would harmonize with Weber's earthy woodcuts and poems. This typographic approach would be called "allusive." I soon forsook attempts at allusive design, preferring a straightforward approach that is considered classic and in the more conservative literary tradition. Of the 350 copies printed, less than 100 were sold. The unsold copies were given to Weber. Recently the book has been sold by rare book dealers at many times its original price.

Meantime, I was not, of course, capable of doing useful work in the composing room of a printing shop, and so I suggested to Mr. Marchbanks that I would like to go forth into the marketplace and sell his printing for him on commission. He told me that one cannot sell fine printing in the usual manner, but I begged to be allowed to try. With rather tired forbearance he permitted this brash and insistent youngster to put together a portfolio of some of Marchbanks' best work. With that under my arm I made innumerable calls on fine furniture shops, publishing houses, banks, foundations, art galleries, and many others who might want superior printing. I seldom got by the pert receptionist whose job it was to send salesmen on their way. Occasionally I would be allowed to meet the person who buys printing. Invariably I was told that they had a good printer and saw no reason for change, especially since it was apparent that the kind of work done by Marchbanks was more

16

expensive. It took three months of dreary refusals and tired feet for me to realize, finally, that Marchbanks was right. Only when I had my own shop did I discover that fine printing is a craft that does not appeal to everyone, and that the person who wants it will make the effort to find the designer-printer. And by the same token, the printer becomes part of that small world of devotees of typography and the craft of the printed book, and there finds his patronage.

THE SPIRAL PRESS

Setting the type for *Primitives* and doing the presswork took all my time, and to Mr. Marchbanks' great relief I gave up my "job." In the meantime a tiny after-hours printing shop had come into existence. The next step, inevitably, was to make a living. I believed then, as I do now, that one should, if at all possible, earn one's living by doing what one enjoys doing. In the pursuit of this conviction I made calls in the book and art worlds. Because I was not now a salesman, but prospecting for myself, I was received with courtesy. At the publishing house of Henry Holt & Company, the production manager, Leonard Blizard, invited me to design title pages for a number of their books. This I did by setting them in type myself in our own small "shop." I showed a finished proof, and when approved, had a plate made to be used by their production printers in those days of letterpress printing. All this I did for three dollars. But it was a start that required the acquisition of some display types and other appurtenances that made it possible to take on small jobs. Thus, hallelujah, I found myself engaged as a typographic designer. It was then possible to make a modest beginning with small equipment, meet with some success, and grow. The time had come to hang out our shingle and look for larger, more interesting work.

Hoffman gave up his position and added his experienced knowledge to my enthusiasms. We became partners, and as work materialized, we bought some power-driven presses, a "stone," quoins, and other necessary printing equipment with mysterious names that had come down from the beginnings of printing five centuries earlier. The "stone" was a heavy machined steel table on which the type forms were planed down and locked for press. A "dummy" and a "printer's imposition" were not what you might think. You could no longer find an upper case of wood for capital letters nor a lower case for small letters, and you might wonder about the real reason for distress when the foreman announced that the shop was out of sorts. Gradually the "art and mystery" became the clear daily job. We went into a lawyer's office and came out a corporation. The sole investment of money in the Spiral Press at its beginning in 1926 amounted to $5,500 for equipment and incidental expenses. All future growth was self-earned. For example, a press could be bought on chattel mortgage with monthly payments over four years. Therefore, if the press was kept busy, it paid for itself.

We needed a name and a mark. I had long been interested in the spiral as one of the basic families of ornament common to most primitive tribes. It is found in nature in many forms—for example, the seashell and the ram's horn. In some early periods shells were used as money, and more important, the design was a symbol of fertility. These were reasons enough. Our mark came from a three-legged, prehistoric Norse triskelion. It was a running figure, too active for a title page. We swung it around, quieted it down, gave it a base, and redrew it somewhat so that it could function in repose in its newly acquired typographic environment. Happy with the mark, the Spiral also became the name of the Press.

George Hoffman, born into a country printing shop in Germany, the son of a small-town newspaper publisher, remembered that he had first set type when he was eight years old. Hoffman went to Bremen as a young man and at an early age became the manager of a sizable printing plant, but he never felt comfortable in striped pants and the German caste system. He came to the

United States around 1920, with his wife and two small children, and began over again as a compositor in a new language. He worked for the Pynson Printers and the Princeton University Press and then became superintendent at the Marchbanks Press. Our meeting there was most fortunate. Without Hoffman's practical knowledge and his excellent grasp of typographic design, my early aspirations would have found rough going—to say the least.

EARLY YEARS

The Spiral Press thrived in its modest way from the beginning. It was my belief in 1926, since strengthened by time, that the market for fine printing is not limited except as it is limited by the capacity to produce it. If there are practitioners capable of doing imaginative work, there will always be people ready and willing to pay for exceptional performance. This was easier when printing processes were more simple, direct, and personal. It must still be true even though physics and chemistry, photography, electronics and the computer have made the production of printing for commerce more complicated in a more complex world.

The Holt publishing house gave us our first real jobs. In addition to title pages, there followed substantial runs of jackets, circulars, and catalogues that formed the first solid foundation for rent and payroll. Among our earliest patrons was the prestigious Knoedler art gallery for whom we produced a number of sumptuous exhibition catalogues, with bibliographies and reproductions. They were expensive. Mr. Henschel, then head of this famous house, believed that if those catalogues made only one or two new friends each year, the money was well spent. I don't know. I hope they did. It can be said with certainty that fine printing does not *outsell* decent printing. The people who buy fine printing and pay the extra cost do so because they care about it for its own sake and for their own personal satisfaction.

Our first large book commission came through the astute art dealer and bookseller, E. Weyhe, who was a benevolent supporter during my typographic beginnings. We had earlier formed a passing friendship when, as a Huebsch salesman, I had sold him some copies of an art book, the work of the painter Abraham Walkowitz. In 1927 Mr. Weyhe had completed arrangements with Adolph Lewisohn to issue a substantial volume about Lewisohn's great collection of contemporary French paintings and sculpture. (The collection was ultimately bequeathed to the Metropolitan Museum of Art in New York.) Mr. Lewisohn wanted his book produced by the formidable Rogers-Rudge combination. But Weyhe insisted on his rights as publisher and promised that his young printer-friend would produce a satisfactory book. It was the first time that I was responsible for handling a manuscript of such importance, with reproductions of famous works of art. With this book—*The Adolph Lewisohn Collection of Modern French Paintings and Sculptures*—I learned the critical importance of proper editing and proofreading. I had every reason to believe that the text we had been given was accurate. Actually it required extensive re-editing. It should be every printer's duty to make certain that what he puts on his presses is really fit to print. It was once standard practice for responsible book printers to have readers on their staffs who were gentlemen of learning, with goatee beards as a mark of their profession, who occupied quiet cubicles where they performed their sacred duties as watchdogs of the printed word. The large Lewisohn book was finished in good time, and one thousand copies were delivered in 1928 to Mr. Lewisohn's expressed pleasure—and to the benediction of the American Institute of Graphic Arts, whose exhibition jury selected it as one of the Fifty Books of the Year. This recognition was an unexpected but most joyous honor for the new young printer.

Random House, established in 1925 (one year before the Spiral Press), became one of our earliest and best customers. Bennett Cerf and Donald Klopfer had bought the Modern Library from the flamboyant publisher Horace Liveright and made it their mainstay for many years. By their own inclinations and through their close association with Elmer Adler of the Pynson Printers, Cerf and Klopfer commissioned and published books of special literary merit in distinguished limited editions. At the same time they became American representatives for the sale of Nonesuch and other European private press books. Among the volumes printed for Random House, the Grabhorn Press in San Francisco produced a monumental folio of Walt Whitman's *Leaves of Grass*, Adler printed his famous *Candide* illustrated by Rockwell Kent, and I was asked to design and print the first collected edition of Robert Frost's poetry. This was an extraordinarily welcome assignment. In the course of its production the *Collected Poems of Robert Frost* became the foundation for a close personal friendship between author and printer that lasted until Frost's death in 1963. Its story will be told in later pages as will the account of the Franklin D. Roosevelt Papers also done for Random House. Meantime at the Spiral Press I designed hundreds of Random House book jackets and other special printed matter. In addition, on a free-lance basis I designed some of their trade books, and redesigned the binding and title pages of the Modern Library in 1939, which lasted until the 1960's. The relationship with Random House continued for about twenty-five years, until they became a publishing empire. Eventually they occupied a fine new building of their own in New York and had annual sales, so Klopfer told me, of one hundred and fifty million dollars during 1978, their fifty-third year as publishers. This incredible growth of a publishing house during one man's working years is symbolic of the half century with which the present book is concerned. Sudden, overwhelming bigness in all areas of life could not be digested within so short a span. Its profound universal effects have, of course, also touched our own world of ink and paper and type.

The day-to-day existence of a small printing house depended on the job printing that came its way with some regularity. Cata-

21

logues, brochures, announcements, invitations, book jackets and record sleeves, bookplates, stationery, and other miscellaneous and promotional jobs provided the wherewithal for the weekly payroll, the monthly rent, taxes, and other insatiable demands. One or more books were usually in prospect and in work. They were best for the printer's soul but somewhat less nourishing for the economic body. However, the ephemera (job printing) received every consideration. In many aspects it is more immediately enjoyable than disciplined bookmaking because one is less restricted in design, choice of paper, color, etc. But ephemera is ephemeral—it usually ends in the wastebasket. Well, not always. Of late, librarians and curators have rescued ephemeral printing for its sociological as well as its typographic importance. The Bodleian Library at Oxford University has long maintained a collection of trade cards and other printed data going back into English history. And only recently the Yale University Library acquired two cartons of Spiral Press ephemera for its Arts of the Book Room.

We spent a maximum of effort on every job, large or small, profitable or not. We followed the precept laid down a generation earlier by Daniel Berkeley Updike for his Merrymount Press. He said they wished to do common work uncommonly well. If asked by a prospective customer to do something I felt was typographically wrong, I refused the work. Herein lies one essential difference between the commercial printer and the printing house. The commercial printer sells to his customer's bidding. The proprietor of the printing house sets the rather inflexible standards of design and production which the customer accepts because that is what he came for.

Fine printing rarely satisfies business people who want big splashy effects. The industrial firms spend money lavishly and expect lavish results. The basic tenets of fine paper with forthright typography do not satisfy where sales are the sole imperative. Nor does business printing satisfy the fine printer. He wants to expend his energies on matters worth printing. Hence the logical tie to cultural institutions who were our mainstay for survival throughout forty-five years.

Within the first two years our plant grew to its approximate final size. We had three compositors, two or three pressmen, and a man who acted as papercutter and shipping clerk. Equipment consisted of an excellent assortment of type for hand-setting, and the necessary appurtenances of a composing room. Linotype and Monotype composition for catalogues and books were purchased from one or two excellent, specialized composition shops that followed our house style and precise specifications. The type in bulk was then delivered to us, and we did the makeup according to design, gave the pages final form, and pulled proofs. The smaller jobs and small books were hand-set in our shop at a time when a comparatively low wage scale made work by hand an economic possibility. Theoretically, there should be no real superiority in hand over adequately controlled machine production. Nevertheless, there is a subtle something—a bit of human warmth perhaps—that creeps into the finished work of the hand. And with hand-set type it is easier to make those small corrections and adjustments that make the difference between good enough and just right.

Press equipment, at the end of our second year, consisted of a Kelly No. 2 cylinder that took a 22 x 34 inch sheet; a 14 x 22 Laureate and a Colts-Armory of the same size; and two smaller job presses for bookplates, envelopes, and the like. Until about the forties it was possible to employ men, called "feeders," who hand-fed the job presses during an eight-hour day at up to a steady thousand impressions per hour. Later, as mechanization spread, the hand-fed presses were replaced by small, automatic job presses. And the Kelly press was much later replaced by the heavier and better Mergenthaler press made in Italy with press-sheet size 22 x 31 inches (competitive with the Heidelberg presses made in Germany); we also had an American Miehle horizontal, 22 x 28 inch sheet size.

During our first year we did not have a secretary or an accountant. As the work increased, it became necessary to have a competent young woman to help with office routine. Because these college girls became our house proofreaders, an adequate education was essential. However, for the scholarly catalogues and books that we produced for cultural institutions we assumed a considerable share of the responsibility for editorial judgment and accuracy, and therefore turned to a learned free-lance reader, Joseph Bernstein, with whom we maintained close relations. A part-time professional accountant was soon needed. Social Security, unemployment insurance, and other paternalistic benefits initiated by the Roosevelt administration have been highly advantageous to society, but they began the avalanche of paperwork from which everyone has since suffered.

Before the enormous expansion of society, our runs were short, our total production small. During our early years we were able to get along on an annual production of less than fifty thousand dollars in sales. By the sixties, in order to survive it became necessary to produce at least three hundred thousand dollars worth of printing annually. Rents, wages, taxes, shipping, pensions, paperwork, and all the other costs of doing business accounted for the increase. But even more crucial were the ever-larger runs of printed matter required by our institutional customers, all of whom had grown beyond belief. The reader of these lines will probably find the figures quoted in this paragraph to be absurdly small. They did not look so to us.

The first four years of the Spiral Press, 1926 to 1930, were also the last years of the affluent twenties. The working conditions of the small printing house had become clearly established. There was a healthy combination of job printing, books for special publishers, and a few books printed and published in the private press manner for one's own indulgence. This was the general pattern, with variations, followed by the several fine printing shops that

24

were set up in the twenties and thirties. As the workload expanded, we found that we needed some twenty-five to thirty orders, large and small, per month, to keep the presses running. That meant, say, three hundred jobs annually, or more than ten thousand assignments over our forty-five active typographic years. Nevertheless, no new work ever left our shop without my planning and direct supervision.

In 1971, when our last job was delivered, it was possible to look back to the privilege of having designed and printed for the Metropolitan Museum of Art, Pierpont Morgan Library, Museum of Modern Art, American Academy and Institute of Arts and Letters, Frick Collection, American Academy in Rome, General Theological Seminary, National Cathedral, Dumbarton Oaks; and for such foundations as the Twentieth Century Fund, John Simon Guggenheim Memorial, Ford, Rockefeller, Carnegie, and Mellon. Among universities, I recall work done for Yale, Harvard, Cornell, Amherst, Syracuse, Indiana, and, happily, the women at Vassar and Manhattanville. Random House, Holt, Viking, Knopf, Pantheon, the Limited Editions Club, and other publishers offered special books and ephemera. Especially close relations existed with the American Institute of Graphic Arts and with the Grolier Club. And there were private collectors, some of whom we will meet before this volume reaches its last page.

THE NINETEEN TWENTIES

New York was an exciting place in the 1920's. That fertile decade witnessed the climax of one typographic era and the beginning of another. Actually, they overlapped. The extraordinary printers, designers, and graphic artists who had begun their careers in the 1890's were at peak performance. We, the new generation, were well aware that we were in the presence of men of conspicuous typographic talents and established reputations. We met them at social and professional functions, visited them in their workshops, studied their printing, used their new typefaces, and treasured their friendships. The most prominent among them were Daniel Berkeley Updike, Bruce Rogers, Frederic W. Goudy, Will Bradley, Carl Purington Rollins, T. M. Cleland, W. A. Dwiggins, Rudolph Ruzicka, and Dard Hunter.

The creative yeast was everywhere at work. A typographic library of considerable proportions was assembled by Henry Lewis Bullen at the plant of the American Type Founders in Elizabeth, New Jersey. George Parker Winship instilled reverence for the printed page in the minds of receptive Harvard undergraduates. Porter Garnett conducted a workshop at the Carnegie Institute of Technology in Pittsburgh, where students set type and printed with due respect for historic principles. Carl P. Rollins wrote a sprightly weekly column about contemporary books and printing in the widely read *Saturday Review of Literature*. Alfred A. Knopf, for the first time in American publishing, issued novels in unusually fresh and attractive formats with colophons to inform the reader about the typeface used in each book. Young men formed new publishing houses—Random House, Viking, Simon & Schuster, and others—who employed a new breed of professional book designers on staff or free-lance. Bookdealer A. S. W. Rosenbach's spectacular acquisitions of rare books in the auction rooms were reported in the next morning's newspapers. Formidable collectors built the Morgan, Huntington, Clark, Folger, and other libraries. And not of least importance were the new, well-to-do collectors, who became the essential audience that bought first editions and press books.

California enjoyed its own typographic and bibliophilic maturity in the twenties with (according to Jake Zeitlin, the California bookseller) "the establishment of great libraries, a thriving antiquarian book trade, book clubs for the support of fine printing, and printers in the tradition of the great masters of the past." The Book

Club of California sponsored an active publishing program for its many loyal members; John Henry Nash captivated millionaires with large and lavish printing; and the Grabhorns came to San Francisco, where they set up their printing house in 1920. Edwin Grabhorn (1890–1968) and his brother Robert (1900–1973), at first influenced by Updike, Rogers, and Goudy, soon developed their own distinctive and distinguished style of typographic exuberance. During forty-five productive years, they printed and published large, colorful books, many of Californiana, for a devoted following of collectors throughout the United States. The active book clubs and other cultural groups on the West Coast also made it possible for several younger printers to make their start, notably Grant Dahlstrom, Ward Ritchie, and Saul Marks.

In Chicago the huge Donnelley organization, printers of national magazines and telephone books, brought William A. Kittredge to Chicago in 1922 to be Director of Design at the Lakeside Press (their division for works of special design) and supported an enlightened program of exhibitions and publications. During the same period a group of printers and graphic artists established the Chicago Society of Typographic Arts for meetings and for displays of contemporary work.

Recovering from World War I, Europe showed remarkable vitality in the arts and crafts. George Bernard Shaw, James Joyce, Picasso, and Matisse were of this time. Great press books came from England, France, Italy, Germany, Holland, and Sweden. New scholarly magazines from several countries fed the excitement. Magnificent handmade papers were still being made in several European centers at prices that made their appropriate uses entirely possible. A surge of new types were designed and cut, and several classic faces were revived for both hand and machine composition by English and European typefounders.

In the United States, in each of the areas related to letterpress printing, such as photoengraving, electrotyping, paper, and bind-

27

ing, individuals appeared for whom craft had special meaning. Paper of real distinction and with a wide range of selection was made by machine at a relatively small mill, the Worthy Paper Company, in West Springfield, Massachusetts, and at the nearby Strathmore mill where some especially beautiful paper was made on their mouldmade machine, a small unit in their big operation. Lewis A. Alliger, a paper merchant in New York, was singularly devoted to the best in paper. Frank Fortney, a gifted young craftsman, soon took charge, and later became owner, of a large bindery in New York, the Russell-Rutter Company, which provided an excellent source for workmanlike binding.

Such, in a few brief highlights, was the stimulating state of the world when those of us who had first smelled printer's ink at the Rudge plant set out on our own in New York. Elmer Adler had already come from Rochester, New York, in 1923 and established his elegant printing house, the Pynson Printers, where he drew writers, artists, publishers, and collectors into his bright bibliophilic orbit. Among the Rudge "alumni," John Fass and Roland Wood started distinguished, if modest, production in the mid-twenties at their Harbor Press; Peter Beilenson, soon joined by his wife, Edna, began a long and productive career at the Peter Pauper Press; Edmund B. Thompson went to a quiet town in Connecticut and printed small books with great charm at the press in his house, which he called Hawthorn House; and I came along with the Spiral Press. Milton Glick at Viking and Melvin Loos at the Columbia University Press were design and production heads; James Hendrickson became a successful free-lance designer.

WHY PRINTING?

Why were we drawn to printing? What are the vagaries of human predilection? We became printers, I believe, because we would find it an occupation that would open doors to the world of books and the arts. It would provide work that was interesting and absorbing, that could be conducted with personal integrity, and that would provide a moderate return for food and shelter. And, withal, there was an intuitive impulse toward craft.

The young people who became involved in the craft and its scholarship did not, of course, fit into a single pattern. Most of those who have succeeded as designers and printers and who have contributed to the arts of the book in our century have come from outside the trade and commerce of printing. They came from varied backgrounds, business and otherwise, they did not wish to follow. There are exceptions, of course. Edwin and Robert Grabhorn worked as compositors in Indianapolis before they began their illustrious career in California; Saul Marks (Plantin Press) first set type in a printing shop in Poland; and John Fass was apprenticed as a compositor in a small town in Pennsylvania. These men started in the trade, but their personal stature and innate sense of design and craft made them rise above the vocational.

The generalities here offered are perhaps inexact, but they do point to the clear fact that fine printing is a cultural manifestation; and that the capacities for craftsmanship and scholarship, when joined together, are among the happy fortuities of the human soul.

SEPARATION OF
PRINTER AND DESIGNER

It will be informative to take a quick look into the past to observe the transition from the practical printer within the shop to the rise of the scholarly young men who established printing houses and to an understanding of their colleagues, the professional typographic designers. During the spectacular first hundred years after Gutenberg, printers were of necessity also typefounders, editors, publishers, and booksellers under one roof. Among the early printers who produced thousands of editions and millions of books, only a handful—Nicolaus Jenson, Aldus Manutius, Estienne, Christopher Plantin, and a few others—enjoyed esthetic talents as well as the capacity to manage a shop and survive in the marketplace. The great folios that we revere today as objects of art are a very small minority among the millions of books printed and published during the fifteenth and sixteenth centuries. The bulk of incunabula is of enormous cultural and historical consequence, but typographically beautiful books are the fewest among them.

The seventeenth century was a bleak typographic period without great men and with few changes in the fundamentals of printing. But during the eighteenth century, giants again trod this earth. Fournier, Baskerville, Bodoni, Didot, Bulmer, and others were responsible for new procedures, sharper types, and noble folios. Until the end of the eighteenth century, printing and its design came from the mind and direction of each individual in his own printing establishment. Mechanization as it developed in the nineteenth century would gradually be responsible for the separation of the designer from the shop. The first historic evidence may be seen in the admirable books of the English publisher William Pickering in mid-century. He was the designer; Charles Whittingham at the Chiswick Press was the printer.

Thus we come to the 1890's, to Bruce Rogers, the first artist-typographer, and to the arrival of the free-lance graphic designers. These men were deeply involved in printing, but they were independent of shop ownership and maintenance. They were the ancestors of all the young men and women of the present century who have become professional typographic designers, whether free-lance, in publishing houses or in advertising agencies. Also out of the late nineteenth century came those three great printers—De Vinne, Updike, and Rudge—who were the prototypes for the smaller, scholarly printing houses that have come along during and since the twenties and thirties.

During the second half of the present century, rebellion against

30

massive industrialism and mechanization has brought forward a fine new crop of workers in the arts of the book who have turned back to pure craft and the dignity of hand labor. Serious and competent young men and women, many associated with college art departments, are printing and publishing interesting and innovative work from type set by hand and printed on hand presses. A few are making their own excellent paper. Participation in printing as a craft and in its design has never been more widespread.

THE AMERICAN INSTITUTE OF GRAPHIC ARTS, NEW YORK

The American Institute of Graphic Arts was the place where the faithful gathered to meet their typographic brethren, where they discussed the many problems of their craft and held exhibitions of significant work. The accepted gospel called for better design and higher standards in the areas of printing. A Board of Directors maintained a headquarters in midtown Manhattan with Blanche Decker as Executive Secretary. Support was provided by individual memberships and by corporate affiliation among concerned publishers, and the manufacturers and purveyors of pertinent materials and services.

Membership came chiefly from the East, but since exhibitions and other activities were national (and occasionally international) in scope, the country as a whole was well represented. During the twenties, membership was counted in the hundreds, but this multiplied in later years as the Institute grew in size and scope.

As a cultural institution, the AIGA achieved its purposes through exhibitions of distinguished work, lectures, workshop courses, plant tours, illustrated catalogues, etc., etc. The juried show, "Fifty Books of the Year," which has been held since 1915, was usually the pivotal annual event. To have one's work chosen was, certainly, the heart's desire of every book designer on the American continent.

After opening in New York, the fifty books traveled to museums, libraries, and other book groups throughout the United States. And for a few years the Department of State sent two complete sets abroad as aids in its efforts to spread American culture and goodwill in the world. Other exhibitions were concerned with printing for commerce, children's books and textbooks, book and record jackets, prints and printmaking, etc. Illustrated catalogues accompanied the major shows.

We all took part, cheerfully and with some conviviality, as volunteers in the selection and mounting of exhibitions, and in the preparation and printing of invitations and catalogues. This was duty and pleasure well mixed among one's colleagues. There was no scarcity of volunteers in the years before World War II. But this too has changed. Paradoxically, it seems that in those years there was less money and more time. Now there is more money and, seemingly, little or no time. At least, little time to give.

The American Institute of Graphic Arts was founded in 1914, when President Woodrow Wilson requested the National Arts Club in New York to make a selection of American books worthy of being sent, at their invitation, to the Leipzig International Book Exhibition. A number of the Club's members, known as the Graphic Group, had already been meeting together. Among them were printers Marchbanks, Rudge, and Norman T. A. Munder; type designers Goudy and Cooper; art director Cyril Nast; magazine editor and historian of printing John Clyde Oswald. The Club turned to this group to form a committee and a jury of selection. After completing their assignment but before disbanding, they founded the American Institute of Graphic Arts and started the "Fifty Books of the Year" exhibitions.

The books sent to Leipzig were, as was to be expected, the work of Rogers, Updike, Goudy, Rudge, and their contemporaries. Their special editions continued to dominate the Fifty Books shows until the new printing houses came along in the twenties and when, too, the books of the general trade publishers showed new life. The importance of attractive books from the young breed of professional book designers was recognized, and trade books occasionally dominated the shows. New university presses and other cultural institutions came forward with greater efforts in the design and production of their scholarly publications. There can be no doubt that these annual exhibitions did much to improve taste and production. They were highly competitive; they stimulated excitement and controversy—all to the ultimate common good.

I served on innumerable AIGA committees, on juries, as editor and printer of their occasional *Journal*, and for some fifteen years on the Board of Directors. Board meetings were usually interesting and provocative as evangelical members wanted everything employing type or lettering to be in good taste. A proposal was even made for better-looking automobile license plates. Alas, the authorities were unmoved.

It is a pleasure for me to remember that in 1952 I was awarded the Institute medal for "craftsmanship in printing." This annual recognition had a distinguished roster of practitioners going back to Updike in 1922, and I was, of course, proud to see my name among them. (Toward the end of my career the Boston Society of Printers made me an honorary member of their respected, long-lived organization.)

During the 1960's the AIGA came into the hands of industrial and advertising art directors and designers. The emphasis thus shifted to promotional printing, and proportionately less attention has been paid to the literary book. I have often wished that the name, chosen in 1914, had been less all-embracing. Perhaps a name related more closely to the arts of the book would have kept the organization more nearly on course.

GERMANY AND HOLLAND

In 1928, when I had been a printer for two years, a major exposition of printing machinery in Cologne, on the Rhine, which included an international exhibition of contemporary typography, drew me to the land that was the birthplace of printing. After Cologne it would be only a short distance up river to Mainz, where a little more than five hundred years ago human ingenuity had resolved the many problems and processes that eventually came together as printing. I wanted to walk the streets of the city where Johann Gutenberg had spent so many years of inventive genius in the pursuit and ultimate realization of a vision that provided the means—the potential—for the dissemination of knowledge to the whole of society. And let us remember with reverence that the Gutenberg Bible, with its 1286 folio pages, its majestic beauty and its incredible perfection, remains today the noblest monument of the printer's art.

Reaction to the long years of ornate Victorianism brought welcome change almost everywhere. In Germany the rather short-lived art nouveau (*Jugendstil*) of the turn of the century was followed by severe "functionalism." This thrust toward modernism spelled the end of the awkward Fraktur type, with its vestiges of gothic, which had dominated German printing since the fifteenth century. Fraktur was replaced by the roman alphabet that had long been dominant in the western world. Its adoption in Germany brought an outburst of new type design to fill the void. This activity was much in evidence at my next stop, the Bauer Type Foundry in Frankfurt. This and a number of other such foundries were cutting and casting excellent new faces by designers whose names had begun to cross the ocean: Lucien Bernhard, E. R. Weiss, Paul Renner, Rudolf Koch, and others.

Across the river Main, in Offenbach, I was fortunate to find Rudolf Koch in his studio at the famous arts and crafts school where he

34

was surrounded, in the ancient guild manner, by a group of brilliant and devoted students. Among them were Fritz Kredel, who later emigrated to the United States, and Warren Chappell, American graphic artist at the workshop for a period of study with Koch in 1931/32. Koch combined a profound reverence for medieval craftsmanship with an understanding of the aspirations of his own time. He regarded the alphabet as one of mankind's supreme, mystical achievements. He had already completed several typefaces that were cut and cast at the Klingspor Type Foundry in Offenbach, one of which (called Eve in the U.S.A.) we already had bought and used at the Spiral Press. Koch, with his students, drew the forms of the alphabet to decorate and honor paper, vellum, wood, metal, textiles, and stone. Instead of a brief visit, Koch kept me much of the day. At first sight he looked like the little men who inhabit enchanted German forests, but very soon he appeared tall as his inner light glowed with his art and his ability to communicate spiritual values through his beautiful work.

My next objective was the Bremer Presse in Munich. William Morris, his Kelmscott books, his romantic philosophy of workmanship, and the sumptuous volumes of the English private presses had found zealous followers on the Continent. The Bremer Presse was one of two German private presses in the grand manner. It was directed by Dr. Willy Wiegand, son of a wealthy German industrialist, and supported by subscription from three hundred bibliophilic subscribers. I was already somewhat familiar with Wiegand's impressive books and with the four typefaces he had designed. His volumes—ultimately ninety-two publications—were the world classics of literature and thought. His folio Bible was printed in his Bible type; Dante and Goethe in his "Latin" (which we call roman); Homer in the Greek font; a missal in Liturgica. The only embellishments were the splendid initial letters drawn especially for each book by Anna Simons. She had been a student in England of the legendary master of letter forms, Edward Johnston.

When I hesitantly phoned one mid-afternoon, Wiegand said, "Of course, come right over." As memory serves me, the Presse was on a side street in a small building of its own. The equipment was on the main floor, and as one entered the workroom a sense of ordered activity was immediately apparent. There were three or four compositors setting type by hand, and pressmen with their helpers working on three or four hand presses with tympans raised and lowered in slow, measured rhythm as the dampened sheets were fed into the presses. I recall two standing presses with stacks of felts used for dampening the handmade paper that was made especially for Wiegand by the Zanders mill in Cologne. Late in the afternoon Wiegand invited me to his office on the floor above, a small room lined with books. He brought out an ancient Spanish sherry, and for the next hour we talked about books and printing. Some of the spirit of the Renaissance survived here in the man and his work.

Unfortunately I was not able to visit the Cranach Presse and its proprietor, Count Harry Kessler. Kessler was a scholar, a diplomat, and an urbane cosmopolite. (He was said to be an illegitimate son of the German Kaiser.) Among many remarkable books that came from the Cranach Presse, Kessler's masterpiece is, I believe, the *Eclogues of Virgil* (1926), with marvelous woodcuts by the French artist Aristide Maillol. This volume, with its paper handmade by Maillol's nephew, also engaged the talents of several Englishmen, including Eric Gill, Emery Walker, and Edward Johnston. Established in Weimar in 1913, the press was closed in 1932 when Kessler was forced to flee from the Nazis.

Leipzig, home of the great prewar international book fairs, was also an important typographic center. I visited the famous graphic arts academy there, and the printing house of Poeschl & Trepte, a fine commercial establishment. During this period several German publishing houses, notably the Kurt Wolff Verlag and the Insel-Verlag, turned out handsome trade books.

The Netherlands has had a distinguished history in the field of type design. England, and especially the Oxford University Press, leaned heavily on Dutch designers and craftsmen during the eighteenth century. I sought out S. H. De Roos, a Dutch painter, who had established his private press where he designed and printed some fine books in the classical tradition. He had made a typeface for his own use and designs for type commercially issued by the Amsterdam Type Foundry. Of special pleasure was a visit to the ancient and honorable Enschedé Foundry in Haarlem, where Jan van Krimpen was the type designer. Van Krimpen's types—Lutetia (which I used with much pleasure for several years for our books and ephemera), Spectrum, Romanée, and others—were among the best of the century. So ended a fine trip, the first of many to Europe, its designers and printers.

ROBERT FROST
AT THE SPIRAL PRESS

From our first years the books made at the Spiral Press led to professional and personal friendships with artists and writers that have been among the richest rewards of a long life. I printed books of poetry for the publishers of Robinson Jeffers, William Carlos Williams, W. H. Auden, Pablo Neruda, and others. But books by Robert Frost were different. They led to a wonderful relationship with the poet that began in 1928 and ended only with Frost's death in 1963. The start was made in the years before the Depression, when Random House published a number of fine limited editions, as well as the very popular Modern Library. Arrangements had been made by Random House with Henry Holt & Company, Frost's publisher, for Random House to issue a limited edition of one thousand signed and numbered copies of Frost's collected poetry. Plates of the type pages of the limited edition, after our printing, would be delivered to Holt, then turned over to their manufacturing printers for the large trade run. When Bennett Cerf invited me to design and print

37

the *Collected Poems of Robert Frost,* I was overjoyed for I had long been a Frost reader and admirer.

The copy for setting consisted of previously printed pages with a few scattered corrections written in, plus a few hitherto unpublished poems. There would be approximately 350 printed pages. I planned it for setting by hand in the handsome van Krimpen Lutetia type. At that time, setting verse by hand was not the prohibitive expense it became in later years. I had thought we would be able to purchase enough type to set half the book. We would then make electroplates, distribute, and reset. But for some reason, we could obtain only enough type from the importers to set about thirty-two pages. It was a cruel blow because reading ten separate sets of proofs would add endlessly to Mr. Frost's labors. I spoke to Cerf about this, but he said the problem lay between Mr. Frost and me and that I should write the poet directly. On explaining the situation to Mr. Frost, I received from him two letters dated 14 February and 18 February 1930:

> Let's see, at thirty pages a shipment, there'll be at least ten of them, won't there? That is going to be a tremendous strain on the weakest part of my nature. But Mrs. Frost and I are both delighted with the pages you have let us see. I shall have to show my appreciation by doing my part.

He closed the second letter with:

> I'm enclosing copies of all the extra poems that get by me at present. If any more do later, they'll go late in the last book.
>
> You may not know it, but my sympathies have been enlisted on the side of small presses and hand setting. My heart will be with you in your work.

With this encouragement we went ahead with composition in Lutetia. But after the second batch of proofs Mr. Frost threw up his hands. He wrote:

> I like an exact text as much as anybody but I should hate to have it left too much to me to achieve one. I reread my own

38

poems, when I have to, with a kind of shrinking eye that doesn't see very well. I don't know if it's inattention I suffer from. It may be love-blindness.

To resolve the situation I suggested that except for the new poems we would not send him proofs at all, but assured him the most thorough reading possible. The readers would be Random House, Holt, our own staff reader, a free-lance editor-reader, and a rather inadequate reader, myself. We agreed to refer to Frost only queries the readers might raise, but mine was the only query. In the dramatic poem "Maple," father and grown daughter talk, and question why the mother, who died just after seeing her infant daughter, named her for a tree. One line read: "Her mother's bedroom was her father's still." These were prohibition years when illegal whiskey was in the news, so I queried the "still." Frost changed the line to "Her mother's bedroom was her father's yet." But fortunately "yet" was later changed back to "still," and so it is still being printed at this writing when Frost's poetry is being bought and read far more widely than during his lifetime.

Paper for the *Collected Poems* was ordered from the Pannekoek mill in Holland with a Spiral watermark. It was a fine, tough, laid sheet, mouldmade, on which no available American ink would lie flat and smooth. After experimentation, a new ink was finally made that we named "Frost Black," with adequate viscosity, without shine, with depth of black and printability. It became well-known as a superior ink, profitable for the manufacturer. Most of our inks were made for us to our own printing needs. I learned that good inks, perhaps like good cheese and wine — and some people — improve with age. So we used only vintage inks that remained on our shelves for a year or more before we used them. (We had a vintage burgundy, but not for drinking.)

The *Collected Poems* was finally printed and bound. To my knowledge only one error was ever found. On page 128 "faces" became "laces" because a plate had been damaged and the letter incorrectly replaced. Nevertheless, Frost wrote in my copy: "To Joseph Blumenthal, who thus in pure bookmaking (nothing added) found things to say that were never said before to my poetry."

During the spring of 1930, with typographic problems resolved and the *Collected Poems* on press, Frost wrote to me: "I hope we may meet sometime soon. I don't like these things done impersonally. Could we induce you up our gully for a day and a night? Or shall I have to come to New York for our better acquaintance?" On a Saturday afternoon not long after receiving that very welcome invitation I took the train to South Shaftsbury, Vermont, to be greeted at the station with simple friendship by Robert Frost's outstretched hand. We were just in time to see some sheep-dog trials a few miles away. Next we drove to the local market, Mrs. Frost's list in hand to pick up food for the evening's meal. And then to the old farmhouse on the hill with its long view to the Green Mountains. That night in the country parlor we sat and talked until two in the morning. Next day we set off after breakfast to take a walk around the farm. It was a warm day, and after only a little while we paused and sat on two adjoining stumps. That ended the tour. We stayed on those stumps and talked until past lunchtime. When we came back late, Mrs. Frost showed not the least surprise.

This encounter with Robert Frost was a wholly new experience for me. I had always thought of myself as a reticent person, yet here I was talking with a great man and a great poet with easy confidence, and completely unselfconscious. I learned, in time, that the sense of elation, the enlargement of the spirit, the evocation of better than one's best, the sense of having given more than one had, all this was a common experience among those who were fortunate enough to have spent some time alone with Robert Frost. Over the years that followed, this freshness of meeting, this re-creation of the spirit, would happen again and again.

For more than thirty years after the publication of the *Collected Poems*, I designed and printed Frost's seven new books in signed and limited editions, a few special publications, and twenty-five Christmas booklets. Before delivery of the manuscript of a new volume to his publishers, Frost would invite me to his home overnight (in Boston or Amherst) and read the new poems to me. The desire to reach out to the person who would give physical form to his words seemed entirely logical to Frost. It did to me, too, and was always an enriching experience.

In 1934 the people at Holt proposed a reissue of *A Boy's Will* in a new, illustrated, but inexpensive, unlimited edition. Frost suggested for a cover "a bristle of three or four scythes, roughly circular as a whole like a handful grab of jack straws." I called in Thomas W. Nason, a New England wood engraver, whose own work was in sympathy with the sparse elegance of Frost's country speech. After a few tries Nason came up with a solution that delighted Frost. For the title page Nason cut an abandoned rural fence post with a vine running through and around it, which became a kind of Frostian symbol that adorned several later pieces of our printing for special occasions, including the program for the Frost memorial service in the Amherst chapel on 17 February 1963.

During the autumn of 1929, before I had met Frost, when the type was being set for the *Collected Poems*, I received permission from his publisher to print his poem "Christmas Trees" as a holiday greeting for my wife and myself. In 1934, when the worst of the Depression was past and the Spiral Press was again established in New York, I asked Frost if he would enjoy having one of his poems used for his, and our, Christmas greeting. He would, selected "Two Tramps in Mud Time," and also requested copies imprinted for his good friend Frederic G. Melcher, the bookloving, printing aficionado, editor of the magazine *Publishers Weekly*. Frost in later years added his daughter, Leslie, and his grandchildren to the imprints that became a family holiday tradition. Frost's publisher, Alfred C. Edwards, head of Holt, Rinehart & Winston, soon came aboard with other Holt executives. Twenty-five titles were issued from 1929

41

to 1962; most of them were first printings of new poems. The climax came with the Holt imprint on the booklets that were sent to the company's friends and customers throughout the country. And together with the Frost family, Melcher, and Blumenthal good wishes, a grand total of 16,555 copies were printed of the last poem, "The Prophets Really Prophesy as Mystics, the Commentators Merely by Statistics." It was Frost's last Christmas. Despite these large runs, few copies have reached the bookstores, but when they do, they justify the line from the early "Christmas Trees," one of the tenets of Frost's philosophy, "The trial by market everything must come to."

Almost all the little booklets were given some gaiety with illustrative decorations by artists who participated in the holiday spirit and received copies with their own imprints. Those who made drawings or woodcuts were J. J. Lankes, Thomas W. Nason, Armin Landeck, Fritz Eichenberg, Joseph Low, Leo Manso, Philip Grushkin, Stefan Martin, Howard Cook, Antonio Frasconi, and Leonard Baskin.

During the later decades of his life, Frost "barded around" the country talking to large and responsive audiences of college students. There were usually several lectures or talks in New York each winter. After his public appearance, he would come to our apartment accompanied by his publisher, fellow poets, and special friends who might have been in his audience that evening. His only food before the reading would have been the yolks of two raw eggs. But at the late gathering in our home he would have a light supper in a separate room, then join his guests to talk for several hours far into the night. This was usually followed by a walk with him to his hotel through sleepy city streets. As I left Robert Frost and returned home, I was well aware that each such evening had been a very great privilege.

THE COLOPHON

An impressive announcement early in 1929 promised a new and exciting hardbound magazine, *The Colophon: A Book Collector's Quarterly.* Its concern would be "with collected and collectible books,—first editions, fine printing, incunabula, association books, Americana, bibliography and manuscripts." The prime mover was Elmer Adler at his Pynson Printers, the splendid, rather personal printing house in New York where the magazine was produced and published. Along with a lively editorial program, fine printing was an integral part of *The Colophon*'s attraction.

In order to enliven the appearance of the magazine and at the same time to lighten his own production load, Adler turned to the best printers in America and Europe to design and print about half the articles in each issue. The major part was done at the Pynson Printers with Adler's vivacious typography. Outside designers and printers were given complete freedom as to arrangement, decoration, selection of paper, etc.; only the 8½ x 10½ inch page size was uniform. Although *The Colophon* could pay little more than out-of-pocket expenses, I doubt that anyone—the famous or the lesser knowns—refused to take part. These jobs were especially welcome during the Depression years when most printing shops had idle time. Contributors included, among others, Updike, Rogers, Goudy, Cleland, Marchbanks, Walpole, Harbor, Colish, Hawthorn House, Spiral and Yale University presses on the East Coast; Lakeside in Chicago; Grabhorn, Plantin, Ritchie, Gentry in California; Francis Meynell, Curwen Press and the printing houses of Oxford and Cambridge universities in England; Clark in Edinburgh; Klingspor in Germany. Given complete leeway everyone produced beyond the call of duty. During its first five years, *The Colophon* thus became an extraordinary synthesis of the imaginative typography of a fertile period.

The men who, as editors with Adler, were responsible for editorial

43

content were John T. Winterich, free-lance writer and man about books; Burton Emmett, bibliophile and head of a large advertising agency; Alfred Stanford, author; and Frederick B. Adams, Jr., collector and, later, Director of the Pierpont Morgan Library.

Until he came to New York City, Adler had been advertising manager for his family's clothing business in upstate Rochester. His contact with layout and promotional printing took a scholarly turn with the acquisition of masterpieces of the printed book. He put his dedication to fine printing on the line when, in 1923, he established the Pynson Printers with type and presses, and solicited work "where quality would not be sacrificed to the exigencies of time and cost." (An independent income was no hindrance, surely, to its faithful performance.)

In his handsome library, designed by Lucien Bernhard, next to the Pynson pressroom, Adler served tea on Thursday afternoons to fortunate acquaintances. One would meet writers, artists, collectors, publishers, printers. This was the era of prohibition when teacups often contained alcoholic refreshment. But to Adler, who neither smoked nor drank, and who had fastidious criteria for people and their ways, tea was tea. I was invited from time to time because I was one of the several young typographers who frequently were called on for *Colophon* printing.

Elmer Adler was one of the people I had approached in 1926, hoping for a job somehow related to printing. He suggested that I make a few layouts from which he could form some judgment. I had never been inside a printing establishment, and what I showed him must have been a sorry performance. Adler took one look and sent me on my way. Nevertheless, three years later he asked me to design and print the opening article in the first issue of *The Colophon*. It appeared in February 1930. The essay, with illustrations, appropriately on colophons, was written by Ruth S. Granniss, the widely loved librarian of the Grolier Club.

The Colophon went through several mutations, a hiatus, and a rein-

44

carnation. The original plan held from 1930 to 1935. From 1935 to 1938, called "New Series," it was wholly produced in octavo at the Pynson Printers with typography by W. A. Dwiggins. In 1939/40 Adler returned to quarto size and called it "New Graphic Series." In 1940 the Pynson Printers brought its notable career of eighteen years to a close, and so temporarily did *The Colophon*. It was reissued in 1948 as *The New Colophon*, published in New York by Duschnes Crawford, Inc., with Adler, Winterich, and Adams repeating very well as editors. The magazine was printed by the Southworth Press in Portland, Maine, in 1948; by E. L. Hildreth & Company, Brattleboro, Vermont, in 1949; by Peter Beilenson in Mount Vernon, New York, in 1950. Thus *The Colophon* came to its end, celebrated and successful in all respects except the financial.

Anyone interested in the adventures to be met in writing, making, collecting, and preserving books—in bookmen's talk—will find enormous pleasure in the many pages of *The Colophon*. They sparkle today as they did fifty years ago.

Other serious journals concerned with books and printing were issued here and in Europe. To anyone interested in typographic history, these magazines are a mine of information concerned with the conditions, the work and the practitioners of the first half of the present century. For the January 1980 issue of *Fine Print* (an excellent journal true to its name, currently published in San Francisco) I wrote an essay in considerable detail on this subject. Here are the names of those publications.

The Printing Art, a lush clothbound monthly publication was issued from 1903 to 1910 with Henry Lewis Johnson as editor. Thereafter it had a varied and less interesting career directed to the trade. *Ars Typographica* was conceived, edited and designed by Frederic W. Goudy, elegantly printed at the Marchbanks Press in New York from Goudy types. Started in 1918, the schedule of deliveries was difficult to maintain, and after a few issues the magazine was enlarged, edited and produced by Douglas C. McMurtrie. *The Book*

Collector's Packet, in pamphlet form from 1932 to 1934, was "A Monthly Review of Fine Books, Bibliography, Typography & Kindred Literary Matters, Edited by Paul Johnston." After two years it was picked up by Norman Forgue in Chicago and succumbed in 1945 to the early death common to all these idealistic journals. *The Dolphin: A Journal of the Making of Books*, was a large, major, scholarly achievement of George Macy at the Limited Editions Club. The first three of the four clothbound volumes that appeared from 1933 to 1941 are, I believe, essential reading for a rounded education in the history and technology of fine printing. *Print*, a "Journal of the Graphic Arts" first issued in 1933, continued to provide a wide range of interests in thirty monthly paperbacks. *Printing and the Graphic Arts*, popularly called *PaGA*, appeared in February 1953 with Ray Nash as the leading editor. Printed at the Stinehour Press, Lunenburg, Vermont, these stimulating booklets survived nine years of quarterly publication.

Several European typographic magazines were read in this country: *The Imprint, Alphabet and Image, Signature* and *Typography* from England; *Arts et Métiers Graphiques* from France; *Gebrauchsgraphik* from Germany; *Philobiblon* from Austria. Most important was the legendary *Fleuron*, the sophisticated soul of the international typographic community in seven remarkable annual clothbound volumes, with scholarly articles on design, type, book illustration, historical research, contemporary biographies, et cetera.

THE DEPRESSION

The Depression that began with the stock-market collapse in October of 1929 did not hurt us at the Spiral Press until a year later. From October 1926 to December 1930 we had had four fruitful years. Starting from scratch, we made a modest living at work we could respect. But with completion of the Frost volume in September, work had fallen off and we were unable to keep our men and machines at work. An unexpected solution presented itself. A newly established printer in New York, anxious to obtain the capabilities of my partner, offered to buy our equipment and take our men if Hoffman would go along. It meant the dissolution of a harmonious partnership, but economic realities were compelling. Furthermore, it fell in with my recurring wish to find a long free period in which to study letter forms and to design a typeface.

Early in January 1931, we paid off the few months of our remaining lease and closed the door on the first phase of the Spiral Press. Another forty years of printed work lay ahead before the door would be closed for the last time.

OF TYPE AND THE ALPHABET

Two weeks after putting the Spiral Press temporarily into storage, with the money received from the sale of our machinery, my wife and I sailed for Europe when ships were the only — and enjoyable — way to get there. The objective would be a new typeface I had in mind. I was well aware that my efforts would not produce the equal of the many excellent types already available. My type might be a poor thing, but it would be mine own. As a designer-printer my business in life had turned to the arrangement in harmonious order of those twenty-six curious forms known as the alphabet. How well did I know them? What better way to arrive at understanding them than to cope with each letter in turn — to draw and redraw and re-redraw each character from a, b, c to X, Y, Z, and the accompanying numerals and punctuation points.

We meet the alphabet as children and accept it as casually as we accept the air we breathe. But the alphabet, a wondrous invention of the human race, did not always exist. It is a relatively recent achievement in the long and dramatic history of man's urge to leave some tangible evidence of his existence on this earth. The first primitive efforts were pictures on the stone walls of caves. Early pictorial representations (pictographs) evolved over the millennia into highly conventionalized ideographic symbols, such as cuneiform strokes baked into clay in Babylonia, and Egyptian hieroglyphics. These abstruse systems were capable of mastery by only a few court scholars and learned priests. Then, along the shores of the Mediterranean, about a thousand years before the Christian era, there appeared a handful of syllabic forms that, marvelously and for the first time, represented the *sounds* of speech. These simple new forms were tied to language, and thereby the written word as a form of communication became limited only by man's capacity to think.

Greece adapted these crude syllabic letter forms from the Semitic aleph, beth, and developed their own more formal alpha, beta. Hence our own alphabet. Subsequently in Rome the Greek characters were refined into the highly sophisticated and majestic capital letters that were chiseled into Roman stone columns.

At the beginning of the Christian era the alphabet consisted only of capital letters (majuscules) laboriously written on vellum by the monks of the early Christian church. With the passage of years, the constantly growing demand for biblical and liturgical volumes and the need to write more quickly gave rise to the rounded characters known as the uncial. These, in turn, evolved into the more easily written minuscules, or small letters. Finally, during the ninth century in the monastery at Tours, under the direction of the scholarly Alcuin, appeared the free-flowing, elegant script known as the Carolingian minuscule. These letter forms then became the dominant book hand in Europe and have survived into our own time without fundamental change.

Five hundred years later Gutenberg perfected the processes of movable type and printing, and completed his magnificent Bible with type simulating the gothic hand then written by German scribes of his region in their illuminated manuscript volumes. The roman letter now in almost universal use in the Western world owes much of its grace to the supremely beautiful writing of the Italian

48

scribes of the fifteenth century—one of the glories of the Italian Renaissance.

Type is the alphabet cut and cast in metal—or so it has been since Gutenberg's legacy to mankind. Although in recent years electronics, the camera, and film have replaced metal type, it is the alphabet, civilization's most precious heritage, which remains the steadfast method of communication. And the book is the prime medium for its preservation.

Two men of genius, Nicolaus Jenson (c.1420–1480) and Francesco Griffo (c.1450–1518), designed the first great roman types. Jenson, a French mint master who had learned about the new craft of printing during a few years spent in Germany, set up his press in Venice. In 1470 he completed the printing of his glorious volume, Eusebius' *De Evangelica Praeparatione*, with type which has since been revered as the most beautiful ever cut and cast. It was modeled, with an eye to the needs of the printed page, on the best examples of the work of the contemporary Italian writing masters. Later in the century, Aldus Manutius (1450–1515), the great Venetian printer, employed Griffo to design several typefaces. Of the greatest importance was the type made for Pietro Bembo's *De Aetna* (1495/96) and an italic first used in the Aldine Virgil *Opera* in 1501.

Jenson's sensitive roman letter and Griffo's sturdy, more workmanlike design are the basic letter forms to which subsequent book types owe their inspiration. This applies to all so-called "old style" faces that grew out of broad-pen forms. Drawn by a pointed pen, the "modern" typefaces, with sharper serifs and greater contrast between thick and thin strokes, evolved, early in the eighteenth century, from the sharpness of copper engraving. During the second half of the same century came the crisp Baskerville and Bodoni types widely in use today. (If Giambattista Bodoni himself were to see the presently available machine versions—perhaps better called perversions—sold in his name, he would be sad indeed.)

Metal type, having served its great purposes, is being superseded

49

by photographic and computer-generated composition. In all probability there will be no more type designed for casting in metal. The old standard faces have been adapted and new faces must be designed for today's several methods that employ the camera. The difference lies in the revolution in the processes of printing. The types of Jenson, Griffo, and their followers were designed for impression into paper with surface texture. Photographic type composition printed by offset-lithography lies on top, without depth, usually on smooth paper without much character. Depth makes the difference. It does in people, too.

In the 1890's and in the early years of the present century, when Updike and Rogers were at the start of their careers, they found few well-designed typefaces available. The same lack existed in Europe. The succeeding decades witnessed a creative upsurge that produced a veritable flood of new types, both for private presses and for general printing. William Morris started the procession with the Golden and Troy types for his Kelmscott Press books. Proprietary house types followed for the Doves, Ashendene, and other English private presses. In 1895 Updike commissioned his first type. It was designed by the architect Bertram Grosvenor Goodhue and appropriately named Merrymount; the second, Montallegro, by the English designer Herbert Horne, was completed in 1904. Rogers designed his Montaigne type for the 1902–1904 Riverside Press three-volume edition, *Essays of Michael, Lord of Montaigne*, and completed his beautiful Centaur in 1914. With the exception of the Centaur, which was later cut and issued by the English Monotype Corporation with some revisions, these proprietary faces were rather mannered and had a dated turn-of-the-century touch. They were rarely used beyond their initial purposes.

In 1913 the American Type Founders broke commercial ground with Cloister Old Style, which was a good but rather archaic rendering of the noble fifteenth-century type of Nicolaus Jenson. It was adopted by John Henry Nash in San Francisco for much of his work, but had only limited trade acceptance. A much more successful effort came in 1916 with a fine recutting of the seminal roman type designed by Claude Garamond early in the sixteenth century in Paris. This ATF Garamond for hand composition was the first complete font I bought for our type cases at the Spiral Press, in all sizes, 8 point to 72 point, roman and italic. A faithful rendering of the same design was put on Intertype, a composing machine similar to the Linotype. I used these Garamonds for much of my early work. My later preferences leaned toward Baskerville and Bulmer, English faces of the eighteenth century, available in excellent, if slightly different, renderings by the American Type Founders for hand composition and on the Monotype and Linotype machines. Other good book faces were available as well, for special moods and needs. In these choices lie the subtleties of book design. However, I cannot state with enough emphasis that what is of first importance is *how the type is used*. If one must make a choice, a poor type well used would be better than a good type poorly used. But who would not wish the right type, rightly used!

In an extremely well-received performance, Frederic W. Goudy produced types in profusion. His most prolific years, wrote Paul Bennett, were from 1911 to 1932 when "he completed sixty-seven designs and produced at least two dozen good, popular types." My own devotion to the Goudy types was less than wholehearted. I found many of his designs soft, especially the popular Kennerley, Italian and Goudy Old Styles, although the Goudy Modern and Deepdene are not subject to this criticism. I bought his Forum and Hadriano inscriptional capital letters, and his black-letter Goudy Text, and found them very useful. The rugged Goudy New Style has survived with honors and has been used to great advantage for hand composition and printing by several of the best craft printers in the recent seventies and eighties.

An innovative program by the Mergenthaler Linotype Company in New York was very successful under the leadership of Linotype's

C. H. Griffith. Excellent new renderings were made of Baskerville, Janson, and other historical classics that were added to old standbys such as Caslon, Scotch Roman, and Bodoni, not to mention the huge Linotype repertory of hundreds of existing fonts, foreign languages, signs, and decorative material. Commissions for new designs were given to two American graphic artists. Dwiggins designed a number of experimental faces of which Electra and Caledonia were issued during the thirties and widely used in American book production. Rudolph Ruzicka designed Linotype Fairfield and Primer. I found Caledonia an excellent bread-and-butter type; the Fairfield is more decorative but serviceable when used with discretion. The Lanston Monotype Company in Philadelphia (unaffiliated with the English Monotype Corporation) was also active during these years but with limited success for its new type efforts. The Monotype was used in the United States chiefly for special composition problems such as tabular matter and fractions.

Of the greatest value to all sensitive areas of printing was a brilliant galaxy of types made available by the Monotype Corporation in London, initiated by the eminent typographic scholar, Stanley Morison. The principal new Monotype revivals of classic models were Bembo, Baskerville, Bell, Fournier, Garamond, Poliphilus, and Blado. Among original Monotype faces by contemporary designers, most significant were Perpetua by Eric Gill, Centaur by Bruce Rogers with Frederic Warde's Arrighi as a companion italic, Goudy Modern by Frederic W. Goudy, Lutetia by Jan van Krimpen, Dante by Giovanni Mardersteig, and Stanley Morison's Times New Roman. Of the twentieth-century designs, only the Times New Roman was a resounding commercial success. Charles Peignot was a courageous typefounder in Paris. A vigorous crop of types were produced in Germany, and others came out of the Netherlands, Sweden, Czechoslovakia, and Italy. Especially noteworthy are several recent excellent types for letterpress and offset by Hermann Zapf, who is also directing his artistry to the new methods of type-

52

setting on film. Many excellent display types appeared in America and Europe, but I have limited these pages to designs intended primarily for book composition.

This is only a sketchy and incomplete picture of the exuberant years of type design and production which provided fresh resources to practitioners of the printed page. With an abundance of classic and contemporary faces readily available, should anyone wish to perpetrate another? I must confess — if confession is in order — that I finally added to the flood with a ripple of my own.

EMERSON TYPE

Instead of being idle in New York during the worst of the Depression, it seemed eminently sensible to employ the sweet uses of adversity to advantage. My proposed type would of necessity be cut and cast in Europe for the simple reason that there were neither craftsmen nor appropriate facilities available in the United States. Innsbruck, a university town in the wonderland of the Austrian Alps, seemed an ideal spot to spend a few winter months devoted not to winter sports but to the elusive forms of the alphabet — to calligraphy and type design. I became immersed in *Writing & Illuminating, & Lettering*, a remarkable book by Edward Johnston, father of the revival of calligraphic handwriting in England. I cut reed and quill pens, practiced on paper and vellum, and imagined myself to be a neophyte medieval scribe. This was followed by photographic enlargements of Jenson, Baskerville, Bodoni, and other seminal type models that I studied and over which I traced for the closest possible familiarity. Finally, after three or four months, with preliminary drawings of a prospective typeface under way, it was time to move to the punch cutter and the Bauer Type Foundry in Frankfurt-am-Main, Germany.

Shortly before leaving our beautiful winter retreat, we were invited to the home of a university professor. At dinner, the companion on my right, a faculty wife, asked if we had been in Innsbruck for skiing. "No," I said, "I am here to design a typeface." "Heavens," she said, "Don't you have any type in America?"

The punches were to be cut by Louis Hoell, then about seventy years of age. He was almost the last of those remarkably skilled craftsmen who, since Gutenberg, had cut punches for type. I believe that the last professional in the United States was Robert Wiebking of Chicago, who cut the Centaur for Bruce Rogers in 1912/13. (However, Wiebking engraved the matrices directly, without punches.) The fundamental process of type design and production changed but little from the fifteenth century until the invention of the Linotype machine in the 1880's. Thereafter machine processes took over. Nevertheless, during the first half of the twentieth century, a few new types intended for hand composition followed early hand methods.

Hoell had cut punches for the Bremer Presse types designed by Wiegand, and I followed their procedures. I sat next to Hoell as he cut and proofed every character every step of the way until the whole font was ultimately corrected and completed. If only for historical interest I believe that the progression from hand-cut punches to matrices should be here set down, however briefly.

The first step was to transfer the drawing, which was about three-quarter inch in height, to the head of a tiny square piece of steel the size of the final type and about two inches long. This becomes the punch when the letter, under a strong magnifying glass, has been cut. The punch is then held in the smoke of a candle that deposits lampblack on its face. When impressed on sensitized paper this becomes a "smoke proof." From this proof the designer gets his first look at the letter he has projected and sees the need for corrections. Corrections and smoke proofs will be repeated until the punch is considered final. After completion of perhaps a dozen small letters and a few capitals, the punches are hardened and then used to strike the matrices in which the type will be cast. With a few pounds of finished type, a few paragraphs were set up and printed to obtain

54

THESE PAGES REPRODUCE WORK
DESIGNED BY JOSEPH BLUMENTHAL AND
PRINTED AT THE SPIRAL PRESS

Primitives (1926). Poems and woodcuts
by Max Weber. The first Spiral Press book.

BAMPENSE KASAI

Mask Bampense Kasai,
Crudely shaped and moulded art thou,
In weighty varied solid frightful form,
Through thy virility brutality and blackness,
I gain insight subtle and refined.
Then 'tis true Kasai that the sculptor in thy making
Was not the jungle savage,
But high spirited and living soul.
In carving thy features Bampense Kasai,
In the crudest geometric form,
Thy savage maker makes an art
At once untrifling big and powerful.
Surely not ignorance but fear and love and spirit high,
Made him make you Bampense Kasai.

The Day of Doom

OR A POETICAL DESCRIPTION OF THE GREAT

AND LAST JUDGMENT

with other poems

by MICHAEL WIGGLESWORTH

Edited with an introduction

by KENNETH B. MURDOCK

With drawings adapted from early New England gravestones
by WANDA GÁG

≻≻≻

Printed and published at

THE SPIRAL PRESS · NEW YORK

1929

Title page (1929). Drawings by Wanda Gág.

This and all other pages here reproduced have been
considerably reduced in size.

THE
POETICAL
WORKS
OF
EDWARD
TAYLOR

Edited with an Introduction and Notes by

THOMAS H. JOHNSON

ROCKLAND EDITIONS · NEW YORK

Title page (1939).

Davy Crockett
AMERICAN COMIC LEGEND

Selected and edited by Richard M. Dorson. With
a foreword by Howard Mumford Jones. Printed at
the Spiral Press for Rockland Editions, New York

Title page (1939). Woodcuts reproduced from
nineteenth-century American periodicals.

BR MARKS
& REMARKS

The marks by BRUCE ROGERS, et al.

The remarks by his friends: H.W. Kent,

J. M. Bowles, Carl Purington Rollins,

David Pottinger, Christopher Morley,

James Hendrickson & Frederic Warde.

❧ The whole gathered and published

by The Typophiles in New York, 1946.

TITLE PAGES FROM
TYPOPHILES CHAP BOOKS

An inquiry into the
MARITAL STATE *for the* DELECTATION
of the FAITHFUL, *written by T. M. for*
Atkinson's Saturday Evening Post of
April 19, 1834, appropriately titled

ON CONJUGAL FELICITY

with an introduction by
HERBERT HOSKING
and homilies elegantly embellished by

EDWARD A. WILSON	WARREN CHAPPELL
VALENTI ANGELO	RAYMOND LUFKIN
ROBERT FOSTER	FRITZ KREDEL
JOHN AVERILL	ALLEN LEWIS
FRITZ EICHENBERG	

privately printed for
THE TYPOPHILES · NEW YORK
MCMXLI

THE
GROLIER
CLUB
1884–1967

AN INFORMAL HISTORY BY

JOHN T. WINTERICH

THE GROLIER CLUB · NEW YORK

MCMLXVII

Title page (1967).

GROLIER

75

A BIOGRAPHICAL RETRO-
SPECTIVE TO CELEBRATE
THE SEVENTY-FIFTH ANNI-
VERSARY OF THE GROLIER
CLUB IN NEW YORK

Title page (1959). Calligraphy by Philip Grushkin.

ROBERT FROST

AND THE

SPIRAL PRESS

Wood engravings by
Thomas W. Nason.

ON
MAKING
CERTAIN
ANYTHING
HAS
HAPPENED

BY ROBERT FROST

COVERS FOR ROBERT FROST
CHRISTMAS BOOKLETS

Drawings by Armin Landeck.

Woodcut in two colors by J. J. Lankes.

THE PROPHETS
REALLY
PROPHESY AS
MYSTICS
THE COMMEN-
TATORS
MERELY BY
STATISTICS

Cover in
Michelangelo type.

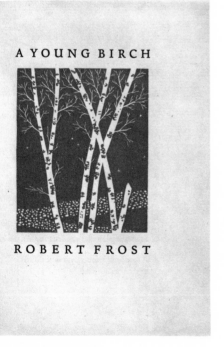

A YOUNG BIRCH

ROBERT FROST

woodcuts by Joseph Low.

MY
OBJECTION
TO
BEING
STEPPED
ON

Wood engravings by Leonard Baskin.

OPEN
SPACE
IN URBAN
DESIGN

A Report prepared for the

Cleveland Development Foundation

sponsored by the

Junior League of Cleveland, Inc.

CLEVELAND · OHIO · 1964

Title page (1964).

on which would be inscribed the

Ten Commandments. But he had

failed to remember that the tables

would be shattered by Moses.

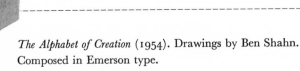

The Alphabet of Creation (1954). Drawings by Ben Shahn.
Composed in Emerson type.

Linoleum block by Antonio Frasconi
from *Twelve Fables of Aesop* (1954).

THE FROG

UPON THE FROG

The frog by nature is both damp and cold,
Her mouth is large, her belly much will hold;
She sits somewhat ascending, loves to be
Croaking in gardens, though unpleasantly.

COMPARISON

The hypocrite is like unto this frog,
As like as is the puppy to the dog.
He is of nature cold, his mouth is wide
To prate, and at true goodness to deride.
He mounts his head as if he was above
The world, when yet 'tis that which has his love.
And though he seeks in churches for to croak,
He neither loveth Jesus nor his yoke.

John Bunyan, *Divine Emblems*

A Bestiary (1955).
Compiled by Richa
Wilbur. Drawings
by Alexander Cald

WE OBSERVE TODAY NOT A VICTORY OF PARTY BUT A CELEBRATION OF FREEDOM —SYMBOLIZING AN END AS WELL AS A BEGINNING—SIGNIFYING RE- NEWAL AS WELL AS CHANGE. For I have sworn before you and Almighty God the same solemn oath our fore- bears prescribed nearly a century and three-quarters ago.

The world is very different now. For man holds in his mortal hands the power to abolish all forms of human poverty and all forms of human life. And yet the same revolutionary beliefs for which our forebears fought are still at issue around the globe — the beliefs that the rights of man come not from the generosity of the state but from the hand of God.

We dare not forget today that we are the heirs of that first revolution. Let the word go forth from this time and place, to friend and foe alike, that the torch has been passed to a new generation of Americans — born in this century, tempered by war, disciplined by a hard and bitter peace, proud of our ancient heritage — and unwilling to witness or permit the slow undoing of those human rights to which this nation has always been committed, and to which we are committed today at home and around the world.

Let every nation know, whether it wishes us well or ill, that we shall pay any price, bear any burden, meet any hardship, support any friend, oppose any foe to assure the survival and the success of liberty.

This much we pledge — and more.

The Inaugural Address of John Fitzgerald Kennedy (1961). Composed in Emerson type. Seal engraved on wood by Fritz Kredel.

All Quiet on the Western Front

by Erich Maria Remarque

With an introduction by HARRY HANSEN
and with illustrations by JOHN GROTH
Printed at The Spiral Press for the members of
The Limited Editions Club · 1969

Drawings by John Groth.

RESURRECTION

A NOVEL IN ● *THREE PARTS*

by LEO TOLSTOY

THE TRANSLATION BY LEO WIENER REVISED AND
EDITED FOR THIS EDITION BY F. D. REEVE
WITH AN INTRODUCTION BY ERNEST J. SIMMONS
AND ILLUSTRATED WITH WOOD ENGRAVINGS BY
FRITZ EICHENBERG

Wood engravings by
Fritz Eichenberg.

THE LIMITED EDITIONS CLUB
NEW YORK 1963

ITALIAN
MANUSCRIPTS
IN THE
PIERPONT MORGAN
LIBRARY

Descriptive Survey of the principal Illuminated Manuscripts of

the Sixth to Sixteenth Centuries, with a selection of important

Letters and Documents. Catalogue compiled by Meta Harrsen

and George K. Boyce. With an Introduction by Bernard Berenson.

THE PIERPONT MORGAN LIBRARY
NEW YORK   1953

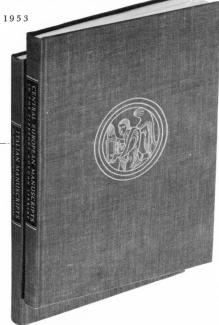

.tle page and bindings of exhibition catalogues
r the Pierpont Morgan Library.

CHINESE

CALLIGRAPHY AND

PAINTING

IN THE COLLECTION OF

JOHN M. CRAWFORD, JR.

NEW YOR

Title and text page for
a Pierpont Morgan Library
publication.

companied by a boy are contemplating the gushing waters. A heavily shaded triangular tip of a large rock in the foreground adds poignancy to the design and the somberness of the setting.

Executed in a sure, broad, and wet manner, derivative in its style and conventional in subject matter, the painting is saved from sentimentality and the danger of triteness by its forthright formalization. To the degree that the design becomes abstract, the human figures become accessorial; no longer do they convey a sense of oneness with Nature or harmonious, blissful companionship with her: small, lean, and tense figures, they seem now almost foreigners, untranslated remnants from the tradition of Ma Yüan and Hsia Kuei, whose landscapes, rocks, and waters are turned into brushwork and chiaroscuro patterns, geometric elements and frozen arcs.

M. L.

32

GENTLEMEN GAZING AT A WATERFALL

Artist unknown; late twelfth to thirteenth century; formerly attributed to Li T'ang

Ink and faint color on silk; fan-shaped album leaf, 9⅞ inches high, 10¼ inches wide

The painting is not signed and bears no seal, nor does any label indicate its Chinese title.

It depicts two elderly men seated on a rock by a mountain pool, quietly contemplating a small waterfall that plunges down on the opposite side of the stream. The waterfall cuts through a gully above which rises a vaguely defined slope dotted with leaves like those of the bamboos on the left side. Presently that slope blends into a summarily outlined hazy silhouette like that of a bulky mountain in the distance, forming the backdrop for the foreground scenery of dark rocks and a neatly defined bamboo grove above them. Distant ranges of undulating hills appear over the slope to the right of the waterfall.

Obviously this fan represents a different school from that which is exemplified by no. 31, where the same theme is treated with formalistic vigor but a loss of warmth and reposefulness. Though less concerned with formal problems, the present painter too is conventional; it would be difficult to discern strongly personal features. Nor is it easy to assign the painting to a closely delimited period. The absence of traits reminiscent of the Ma-Hsia style should favor a later twelfth-century date at the earliest, but it is unsafe to insist on this possibility; a later Southern Sung date, however, appears to be justified.

M. L.

33

STROLLING ON A MARSHY BANK   PLATE 21

Liang K'ai, early thirteenth century

Ink on silk; fan-shaped album leaf, 8⅞ inches high, 9¼ inches wide

This important, austere, and beautiful work, signed by the artist, was previously reproduced in *Ta-feng-t'ang* (vol. IV, pl. 14) under the title *Tse P'an Hsing Yin*, "Strolling and Humming on a Marshy Bank." It does not seem to be recorded, nor does it bear earlier collectors' seals. It is missing in both Tanaka's monograph, *Liang K'ai*, and Sirén's *List*.

[87]

for the first time an idea of how well my drawings had survived transformation into type, how their appearance interrelated with each other, and some feeling for the type in the mass.

Before going on with the cutting of what would become Emerson type, it will be of interest to explain one of the very important fundamental differences between the ancient method of cutting type by hand versus the shortcuts provided by modern mechanical processes. Before the invention of the camera made photographic mechanical reduction and enlargement possible, each letter in every size, from less than 6-point to more than 72-point, was cut individually by the punchcutter. This was a marvel of disciplinary control because the designer-punchcutter could compensate, as he cut, for the elusive optical relations between major and minor strokes, thickness of serifs, etc., which change for each size, however slight. Modern methods make reductions and enlargements from a single pattern. No compensation for distortion or unbalanced relationships is possible. These minutiae are not, of course, apparent to the general reader, but they explain the great vitality of much early type versus the rather static lettering and film type usually seen today.

The proof of the Emerson type pudding was in the printing. On seeing the dozen pieces of type from the first cutting made into a full page and printed on a good sheet of paper I found the overall result (type in the mass) heavy, with the individual characters too designed. Simplification was needed. The punches were recut and a second trial printing made. The direction was right but had not gone far enough. After a third refinement the type had reached the limit of my capabilities. The entire font was then cut and a limited amount of type cast.

I took the final trial run to the Bremer Presse, where they very kindly set and printed complete full-alphabet text pages. There had been an extraordinary transition from the first cutting. The many small corrections in the several stages of development produced a typeface with, so it seemed to me, a character of its own. Since no further changes were to be made, I ordered one thousand pounds of this 14-point font of roman type to be cast at the Bauer Type Foundry and shipped to New York. About nine months had been consumed from the first efforts at design to the finished type.

I brought the punches back with me but left the matrices in Frankfurt for possible future castings. That was 1931, when Nazi brawls were already reported in the newspapers, but the possibility of another catastrophic war in the near future was unthinkable. We were greatly alarmed by Hitler's antics, but our German acquaintances had assured us that he was only a passing phenomenon. How soon they learned otherwise!

On our return we stopped in England where I showed my new type to Stanley Morison at the Monotype Corporation. As a duty to their craft and to their times the enlightened British Monotype management issued a few contemporary typefaces they considered distinguished despite their awareness that designs by living designers were rarely commercially profitable. When Morison and W. I. Burch, Managing Director of this influential organization, offered to add my new and as yet unbaptized type to their superb repertory, I was astonished and deeply moved. The italic had not yet been designed, and I asked for time to respond to their flattering proposal, although I felt certain that I would accept. For payment they suggested a token of ten pounds sterling (then fifty dollars) and a royalty of two percent on sales of matrices. But Morison warned me not to anticipate riches. He was right.

Burch and Morison invited me to join them on a visit to the Monotype plant in Surrey, where type was cut and cast and where the machines were built. It was about two hours from London, and we drove down by car. On the way I learned that in off-hours Mr. Burch was a painter and exhibited his work (as did Winston Churchill) at the annual exhibitions of the Royal Academy. Arriving at "the works," as the British called it, we went directly to a small wainscoted dining room where I experienced British courtesy and hospitality. Waiting around the table were the plant's six or eight department heads, gathered over a simple but slightly ceremonial shop luncheon, to greet the visiting designer from overseas whose work they would one day bring to completion. Friendly professional warmth was exchanged all around, and this American left England a few days later even more Anglophilic than before.

During this London visit I found Bruce Rogers at his favorite, small, Dickensian Hotel Anderton in Fleet Street. At dinner in one of his favorite Italian restaurants in Soho, I was overjoyed when he invited me to join him on a weekend trip to the Oxford University Press, where his Bible was then in progress. We put up at the Golden Cross in Oxford, which Henry Kent called "one of the properest inns in all England . . . once within, you find yourself, in time, back two or three centuries." On Saturday night we went to the local music hall, where the great English favorite, Stanley Holloway, was singing. The scholarly John Johnson, Printer to the University, whose reputation I knew, conducted me through their modernized ancient plant. On later journeys to England I was fortunate in visits to Cambridge, where Brooke Crutchley, Printer to Cambridge University, and John Dreyfus, his associate, showed me their plant and began friendships that were often renewed when they came to the United States.

Back in the United States I showed proofs to C. H. Griffith at the Mergenthaler Linotype Company. To my great surprise he suggested that Mergenthaler would like to purchase my type design and make it available for Linotype composition. Asked about terms, Griffith offered a flat fee of five hundred dollars without royalty. Even during that Depression year (1931) I found the offer inadequate. I recalled that Goudy had told me that he had sold his designs for fixed sums without royalties and never benefited, as he should have, from some of his very popular types. I had no illusions about the possible success of my typeface. Nevertheless a royalty arrangement seemed a self-respecting gamble even if a poor one. So I wrote

57

to Morison that I was proud to accept the Monotype proposal. The name and an italic would soon follow.

The font that had been brought from Germany consisted of individually cast characters for hand composition, normally called foundry type. Because the infant needed a name we called it "Spiral." But once the Monotype version would be offered to the public and once designers would, hopefully, wish to refer to it, a more distinctive name was desirable. The type's debut was made via Ralph Waldo Emerson's 1836 essay, *Nature*, which we set, printed on the hand press, and published at Croton Falls, New York, in 1932. I chose this great piece of American prose not only for its brevity and literary substance, but also for its long unbroken paragraphs that would show the type to best advantage. And as an extra bounty, the type was baptized with Emerson's illustrious name, albeit without his knowledge and consent. But I hoped that he would have given his blessing to this somewhat quixotic American undertaking.

The Monotype craftsmen made an extraordinarily faithful copy of the original 14-point foundry type for their own 14-point. Careful proofs were sent to me for approval for this and all other details and sizes. Comparing letter for letter, the two 14-point versions seemed identical; the differences, if any, were not discernible to me. But sharp-eyed aficionados of this esoteric fragment of civilization say that the foundry type does have more refinement. I suspect that its subtle superiority lies in the greater hardness of its metal, which will give more crisp and incisive depth to the printing, especially if done on fine paper. Also there is some advantage in the fitting of foundry type (the microscopic spacing between letters) versus the limitations imposed by the machine.

The Monotype Emerson's first use was in the Coronation program in Westminster Abbey of George VI in 1937. The program was printed by Eyre & Spottiswood, prepared by Stanley Morison. Monotype Emerson, roman and italic, was finally issued in 8, 10, 11, 12, 14, 18, and 24 point. It was included in the company of

58

venerable types of the past and present in a booklet issued by the Monotype Corporation, *Twenty-one Classic Typefaces for Book and Periodical Setting on Monotype Composing Machines.* A subtitle added that these types were "Selected from a repertory of over five hundred series as timeless masterpieces of type design which will remain in distinguished use for generations to come." Before the arrival of the computer this statement did not seem too outrageously optimistic.

As predicted, Emerson type was not a commercial success although it has had somewhat of a following. Nevertheless, I enjoyed the experience involved in its making and have had pleasure in using both versions where appropriate. It may not be a versatile, bread-and-butter face; it is perhaps too close to Renaissance classicism, and if time and opportunity had offered, I would have enjoyed a second attempt with a more contemporaneous approach.

After forty years of use, our foundry type was worn. When the Spiral Press finally closed its doors in 1971, the type was consigned to the melting pot as scrap metal—its fortissimo grand finale. The type I gave to Victor Hammer is still being set by students of printing in Lexington, Kentucky, where Hammer had ended his career. When Hammer arrived in the United States as a Hitler refugee, he preferred the Emerson to any of the types commercially available. In order to help with his start in a new country, I gave him a few hundred pounds of the foundry type before it was available on the machine.

Only the Monotype Emerson remains for the present and the future, if any. The original punches cut by Hoell, the smoke proofs he made, and the matrices struck by the Bauer Type Foundry (which survived World War II bombs) have been acquired by Rochester Institute of Technology's School of Printing for the Melbert B. Cary, Jr., Graphic Arts Collection. There, I hope, future students of the craft will find these artifacts of historical interest.

PRINTING ON THE HAND PRESS

In January of 1932 we returned to a United States paralyzed by the Depression much as it was when we left it a year before. Unemployed men were selling apples on street corners at a nickel apiece, savings were fast disappearing, breadlines were longer. There was then no unemployment insurance, no social security, no Medicare.

It would have been folly to reestablish the Spiral Press in New York with such conditions prevailing. Besides, I had a thousand pounds of new type that wanted using. Until circumstances would again allow good printing, a retreat into a quiet spot in the country, not too far from New York, might provide an opportunity to spend a year or two in a return to fundamentals — to the basic craft of type composition and printing by hand on dampened handmade paper. At that period when competent type composition could be produced on Linotype or Monotype machines, and when letterpress printing was the order of the day, a turn back to primitive methods might seem to be dilettantism. Actually, it was not.

There is a rare spiritual lift to articulate hand labor in the pursuit of craft in association with a meaningful text. One of the great rewards is the profound satisfaction of seeing crisp, sparkling type pages coming off the hand press on exquisite dampened handmade paper. Such printing is not a normal means of economic subsistence, but where its practice is possible, it is a profound humanistic experience. Furthermore, the intimate contact with ink and paper and impression provides an understanding of the affinity of type to paper not otherwise obtainable. Such knowledge will serve the designer who also depends on the more remote control of automatic machinery. Lewis Allen, with his wife Dorothy, has devoted himself to printing and publishing splendid books on their hand presses in California. He has written, "One of the supreme pleasures available to man is intelligence, discipline, and knowledge guiding the hand to create beautiful as well as intellectually desirable objects; and this

60

pleasure is uniquely inherent in the handpress." And it is a pleasure to add that one of the masterpieces of bookmaking of our time comes from the hand press. It is *Granite and Cypress* by Robinson Jeffers, designed by William Everson and printed by him with his students at the Lime Kiln Press of the University of California, Santa Cruz. It was completed in 1975.

Committed to the hand press, I found a house overlooking the rolling hills of Westchester beyond commuting range, in the small town of Croton Falls, New York. The new home had a daylight basement with concrete floors suitable for presses and big laundry tubs that we would use for wetting the felts for dampening paper. In order to do some bookmaking, a few printing assignments would be needed. Then it would be possible to build up a small staff. George Macy at the Limited Editions Club (of whom more later) offered me *The Lyrics of François Villon* with two-color woodcuts by Howard Simon. In an edition of 1500 copies this was a considerable challenge. Macy had already completed arrangements with Eric Gill to illustrate and print an edition of *Hamlet* on his hand press at High Wycombe in England and expressed pleasure that there would be two books set by hand and printed on the hand press for his 1932/33 list. A few other smaller commissions came along later.

Two weeks that I had spent as a guest at the Bremer Presse in Munich observing their processes were now of utmost benefit. Finding hand presses in workable condition would be the first requirement. The earliest printing presses were modeled on the wine presses used along the Rhine River in Mainz, where Gutenberg printed his Bible. They were of heavy wood with a positive screw action, turned by a sturdy bar that drove down the platen for the impressions of inked type against paper. Fundamental changes were few until the Stanhope iron press was made in England about the year 1800. By the middle of the nineteenth century several iron hand presses of advanced design employing levers and toggle joints were manufactured—chiefly the English "Albion" and the American "Washington." R. Hoe & Company of New York produced more than six thousand Washington hand presses, most of which were junked with the introduction of motor-driven automatic presses. Some were still used during the early years of the present century by photoengraving houses as proof presses, and it is these that have been rescued by craft printers. I located two Washington presses in New York. There was need, too, of some large two-handled rollers for inking the type forms, and of one or two lithographic stones that are ideal surfaces for rolling out the ink. A standing press would be useful when dampening paper. Type stands and the other usual appurtenances of a printing shop were acquired and brought to Croton Falls. When, during that Prohibition year, an open truck with these strange-looking objects drove up to our new home, our neighbors had serious misgivings that a bootlegger had come to town. Some weeks later, when the shop had been put together, the local minister called and was relieved to find that our presses squeezed out nothing more intoxicating than the heady words of a French poet who lived many years ago.

Our staff consisted of a compositor and two pressmen who had been idled by the Depression. They were helped by two local boys who pulled the press levers, washed rollers, and did other clean-up jobs that had been done by printers' devils since ink first soiled a printer's hands. This completed our staff if I may be included as a pinch hitter wherever needed, and including my wife who hung the sheets in the attic to dry and made lunches five days a week at twenty-five cents each. This being Depression time, twenty-five cents provided ample fare for hungry workers. Before proceeding with Villon's Gallic lyrics, we set and printed the Emerson *Nature* in an edition of one hundred copies on dampened "Maidstone" paper, a beautiful sheet handmade in England. The books were hand-bound by Peter Franck.

One of the subtle goals to be sought in bookmaking is a smooth, even page of type composition. Bruce Rogers said that the decorative value of a simple page of beautiful type, beautifully printed, is a value quite apart from the esthetic pleasure given us by any other of the graphic arts. The choices open to the designer seem to be few —selection of typeface and its size, length of line, spacing between lines, a running head, page numbers, margins. But the manipulation and disposition of these units on a page without embellishment can be the mark of genius. If all that we do is a self-portrait, or self-portrayal, there need be no cause for wonder that the sensitive devotee will recognize, in the unadorned pages of a Jenson or Baskerville or Bruce Rogers, the inspired hand of the designer. These are imponderables. They can be experienced; they cannot be described. The results are called art.

For the *Villon*, Macy made the interesting and very appropriate suggestion that the paper should come from the handmade paper mill then recently established by Dard Hunter, the eminent American historian of primitive papermaking. This was the first attempt to make handmade paper professionally in the United States since the first papermaking machines were introduced here in 1817. Hunter was persuaded about 1926 by a young businessman that a market existed for a modest fine paper output. Some years before, when Hunter had been in England, he had purchased a small paper mill about to be dismantled. It was shipped to the United States and stored in the expectation that the craft might one day be revived in this country. By coincidence, an English papermaking family had written to Hunter expressing a desire to emigrate. Hunter yielded. A building that once housed an iron foundry and would be suitable for papermaking was acquired in Lime Rock in the northwest corner of Connecticut, lying along a trout stream that flowed into the Housatonic River a mile away. Local history recorded that cannons for the armies of the American Revolution and for the northern forces during the Civil War had been cast in this mill from the excellent iron mined in the neighboring Salisbury hills.

Unhappily, there were insuperable problems for the Hunter mill.

63

The water supply and other factors, some of them personal, made it impossible to supply clean, uniform, printable paper in daily production. The paper for the *Villon*, a rather large order for this mill, was not acceptable and was rejected with great regret. Soon thereafter, with the Depression adding to his woes, Hunter abandoned the whole undertaking. The equipment was removed and set up as a permanent exhibition at the Institute of Paper Chemistry in Appleton, Wisconsin. The eighteenth-century structure that had housed the papermaking project was swept downstream in the great Connecticut flood of 1955 and disappeared. At this writing, superb paper is again being made by hand in the United States on a modest scale by adventurous members of a new generation.

Fine paper is the absolute prerequisite to fine printing. Fine paper, skillfully made, is a creative artifact, a delight to the eye and a pleasure to the touch. Handmade or mouldmade papers are the only logical choice for work produced on the hand press. When properly dampened, such paper offers a highly receptive surface that permits the ink to penetrate and to produce an incised effect, however slight, that gives depth and an extra dimension to the printed page. Handmade and mouldmade papers are made sheet by sheet and slowly air-dried in contrast to paper made by machine at great speed on a continuous web and instantly dried on heated rollers. Handmade paper has more character than mouldmade, but the latter, from a mechanically operated mould, is more uniform in thickness and surface texture, and thus presents less difficulty in printing. Unless especially soft-sized, handmade papers must be dampened to reduce the resistance to ink of the animal-glue sizing that is added to strengthen and stiffen the sheets. (Dampening machine-made paper would be an absurdity on automatic machinery.)

We dampened handmade paper at Croton Falls with felts, the method used at the Bremer Presse. This was a logical and rather foolproof method for the press at Munich which maintained a considerable daily production on a very high level of expert craftsmanship. But there are simpler methods. Lewis Allen has written an excellent manual, *Printing with the Handpress* (1969), which covers all phases of equipment and processes. He has developed a simple and ingenious method for "damping" paper, which he describes with illustrations. Consequently I shall here forego any further discussion except to add a warning that most beginners make paper too damp. There is a delicate point at which paper has been correctly conditioned for printing. Our rule was that the paper should be dry to the touch and cool to the cheek.

Having rejected the unhappy lot from the Hunter mill, the paper for the *Villon* was finally ordered from the Worthy Paper Company, a small mill in Massachusetts that produced excellent paper. They cared deeply about their output, which included a variety of interesting papers that ran a close second to the mouldmade papers from Europe. (But alas, the Worthy mill was unable to survive competition from the giant papermakers and the commercial trend toward standardization.) Their paper for the Limited Editions Club book met our expectations for receptivity to the type and for the two-color woodcuts that we printed directly from the blocks. It was soft-sized, and there would be no advantage in dampening it.

In designing at Croton Falls, since we had no display types, I had to face the challenge of setting title page, introduction and text all in the one available 14-point Emerson handset type. The result proved what I hope I never forgot—that the best effects are achieved with the fewest possible type sizes. For emphasis one may have a title in large display or some well-chosen and restrained use of color. Elimination of unessentials is the problem. Economy of means is a valuable spur. Dramatic simplicity is a wonderful accomplishment. If any reader doubts the validity of these pious admonitions, I recommend a careful perusal of the works of the historic masters. I would particularly and reverently suggest, in this matter, Bruce Rogers' *Odyssey of Homer*, printed in England in 1932—in my opinion one of the most beautiful books of all time. Except for the book's

65

title and the initial letters at chapter openings, there is only one size of the Centaur type.

Almost a year was needed to set the type for the *Villon* and to print 1500 copies of its 112 ample pages with thirty full-page woodcuts in two colors. A second year saw some miscellaneous work, including two small books for a New York collector, and the design and handsetting in Emerson foundry type of a book, appropriately entitled *Casa Mañana*, for Mrs. Dwight Morrow, wife of the American ambassador to Mexico. She had written a fascinating text about their beautiful home in Cuernavaca and about the Mexican folk art she collected. The book was illustrated by William Spratling. Because of the need for timely delivery, the sheets were printed by my colleagues at the Marchbanks Press in New York.

After two years in a typographic ivory tower, the funds I had received from the sale of machinery and equipment in 1930 were exhausted, and the time had come to face the economic facts of life. Mr. Roosevelt was in the White House, and the nation was going back to work. So, in 1934, I returned to New York.

THE LIMITED EDITIONS CLUB

Over a period of twenty-seven years, George Macy, at his Limited Editions Club, published a book every month—altogether more than three hundred books—in a program that touched every living practitioner involved in the cultural aspects of the printed book. The texts were the classics of literature edited and with introductory essays by prominent literary scholars, illustrated by leading artists, and produced by the best typographic designers and printers on five continents. Editions were 1500 copies mailed to subscribers.

Planning began in the booming twenties, but the first book appeared in October of 1929, the "black month" when the stock market collapse ushered in the Depression. The Club survived the bleak years and continued after Macy's death through several changes of ownership. I will limit this brief overview strictly to the active years of his direction.

In 1959 the Limited Editions Club issued a history of its first twenty-five years (1929–1954) and its first 250 publications in a weighty volume entitled *A Quarto-millenary*, which included essays, copious reproductions of printed pages, a comprehensive bibliography, and illuminating comments by Macy on most of the books. Statistics culled from that bibliography will give some idea of the extent of the program, and it must be realized that Macy was involved in every detail of every book's selection, planning, and production. There were 184 authors, alphabetically from Henry Adams to Émile Zola; 250 editors and translators, Leonie Adams to Avrahm Yarmolinsky; 150 illustrators, Valenti Angelo to Grant Wood (including Matisse and Picasso); 82 designers, Elmer Adler to E. R. Weiss; and 130 diverse printers. The printers, in addition to the Americans, include the venerable Oxford and Cambridge university presses and others in England and Scotland, and one or more establishments in Argentina, Canada, China, Czechoslovakia, Denmark, France, Germany, Italy, Japan, Mexico, the Netherlands, Russia, Sweden, and Switzerland. The bibliography also lists 36 binders, 86 different typefaces, and 57 names of paper manufacturers, hand and machine. Significantly, for the standards of bookmaking maintained, I should point out that Bruce Rogers was called on to design eleven titles, including the 37-volume Shakespeare; Francis Meynell was responsible for seven books; and Giovanni Mardersteig designed and printed the same number at his Officina Bodoni and the Stamperia Valdonega in Verona, Italy. If these three practitioners were the brightest stars in a very productive period in the history of fine bookmaking, there were also competent designers and printers of somewhat lesser brilliance.

In addition to the monthly commitment of books for Limited Edition Club members, the Heritage Club, and two subsidiary book clubs, Macy planned and issued several special publications. Of

67

prime significance to the literature of the craft was *The Dolphin: A Journal of the Making of Books*, in four large volumes from 1933 to 1941. Macy drew on eminent scholars and articulate practitioners for informative essays on every aspect of the esthetics of bookmaking and the techniques of production. Volume three in the series, *A History of the Printed Book*, is the most interesting, the most comprehensive, and the most scholarly work on the subject in a single volume, in or out of print.

George Macy was dedicated to making great books. He combined the spirit of a productive idealist with the practicalities of a hard-headed businessman. This dichotomy was also characteristic of his publishing activities, and therein lay the conflict responsible for the successes and the failures of the Limited Editions Club books. Most of the great books since William Morris have come from private presses conducted by men of wealth or they were produced in printing houses subsidized, or adequately paid for, in one way or another by individuals and institutions. As a publisher, Macy faced the need to make a profit—and he did. His solution at the outset was to find 1500 subscribers committed to take twelve books each year for $120 paid entirely or monthly in advance—a considerable sum in the twenties and especially during the five Depression years. Prices were of course later increased, but were always moderate when compared to the costs of private press books printed in small editions. The books had to be, and always were, of exceptional monetary value.

Salesmanship was necessary to enroll members; survival required that the books attract and hold the membership. How many members bought the books for their artistry and craftsmanship and read them, and how many bought them to show dinner guests their precious shelves of (unread) great literature handsomely printed and decoratively bound? Macy tried to satisfy both groups. This was the flaw in the program that produced some splendid books and others which were pretentious, with typographic extravagance and gadgety bindings. Alas, one may ruefully ask whether magnificently

68

printed books were ever made to be read—or best kept behind glass and admired as precious objects of art. Only a handful of immortals in the history of printing have brought these opposites together in typographic and bibliographic bliss.

My relations with Macy were frequently fruitful, usually difficult, never dull. He was not an easy person as a friend, employer, or client. With only one or two conspicuous exceptions, he was unable or unwilling to hold a key employee more than six months or a year. Withal he was a scholarly personality of wide knowledge and accomplishments, and the years would have been poorer without him. The Limited Editions Club and its related activities were stimulating and valued sources for editors, printers, illustrators, paper manufacturers, and bookbinders. The assignments were almost always welcome and often sorely needed.

I produced six of the books of the quarto-millenary. After Macy's death in 1957, I designed and printed another half dozen when the Club's production was in the capable hands of Max Stein. Three books deserve a few special words. Macy's publications, like his own personality, were rarely cut and dried. The books usually involved situations and problems that could add zest to typographic solutions.

For *Sister Carrie*, the great novel by Theodore Dreiser, with an introduction by Burton Rascoe, Macy had commissioned illustrations from Reginald Marsh, one of America's best contemporary painters with a fine dramatic graphic sense. In most instances Macy had illustrations made before choosing a typographer, thus presenting the designer with the necessity of adapting design to completed pictures. I believe the two elements are best developed in close collaboration between artist and designer. Fortunately, Marsh had prepared nothing in advance and was wholly agreeable to trial and error in achieving a harmonious relationship between type and illustration. After several experimental proofs he finally completed drawings for chapter headings in a crayon technique from which we were able to make excellent line plates that were printed in a rich

69

brown ink. The book set in Janson Linotype and completed in 1939 has been admired and is one of my books that I still enjoy when, late in the night, I lose myself in Dreiser's cumbersome but compelling prose.

My reluctance to accept finished artwork was hardly in order when Macy proposed Blake's illustrations for Bunyan's *Pilgrim's Progress*. The text was edited by G. B. Harrison, with an introduction by Geoffrey Keynes. Macy had persuaded the Frick Collection in New York to allow reproduction of the beautiful Blake watercolors that they owned. It was a brilliant conception to bring these two masterpieces together. Arthur Jaffé in New York made superb full-page, full-color reproductions by his collotype method. The text was set in Monotype Emerson and published in 1941.

A few years later I was bemused when asked to design and print a section of the Talmud, "The Wisdom of the Fathers," in Hebrew and English. This was my first real introduction to the Talmud, which I barely remembered from boyhood Sunday school, and the first time that I met Hebrew type face to face. The available Hebrew on Linotype or Monotype all looked like Kosher delicatessen signs, so I added to my typographic education with a thorough study of Hebrew typefaces of the past and present. Eventually I found a superb new design by the German graphic artist Henri Friedlander, a Hitler refugee who arrived in Israel via the Netherlands and became head of the Hadassah School of Printing in Jerusalem. The type, appropriately called "Hadassah," had recently been cut by Amsterdam Type Foundry, and we were able to import an advance casting. With the help of our Irish compositor we hand-set the Hebraic Talmud laws in the 16-point Hadassah type; the English translation was set in Monotype Poliphilus caps, with the exegesis, or commentary, in Bembo. The editor and translator was Dr. Judah Goldin, Professor of Judaica at Yale University. It was originally planned to have Ben Shahn make the illustrations. Unfortunately a misunderstanding arose concerning lack of artist royalties, and

70

Shahn withdrew on principle. Ben-Zion was then chosen, thus maintaining an all-Jewish cast of characters: authors and commentators, publisher, editor, illustrator, and printer.

James Laver, English author and essayist, Curator of Prints at the Victoria and Albert Museum in London, wrote in 1954: "Indeed, if by any atomic chance all the books in the world should be destroyed except for one complete set published by the Limited Editions Club, the scholars of the future would still possess a most impressive portion of world literature, and would certainly have a very good notion of the work of the best book illustrators of the world during the last twenty-five years." And I may hope that those same future scholars will not overlook the designers, printers, and binders.

WHAT MAKES FINE PRINTING FINE

Sooner or later a concerned person asks the question: What makes a piece of fine printing fine, and how does one achieve it? In a favorable review in the *New York Times*, 23 December 1977, of *The Printed Book in America*, the critic wrote, "I wish that in discussing the individual books, Mr. Blumenthal had told more in detail what made them illustrious and beautiful." Alas, how does one define good taste and the creative imagination? The art historian may have earned the right to rush in, but the practitioner had better watch his step. At the opening of an exhibition of Bruce Rogers' work, he was asked how he arrived at the design of his beautiful books. He replied that he really did not know, but that if he ever found out, he wouldn't tell because then he could never change his mind again.

It seems to me that the capacity for creative design is intuitive, subtle and mysterious. Sometimes the work flows smoothly; sometimes nothing comes out of a laboring mind. Then, when least expected, it can spurt like a geyser. The next day it may look pretty good, or incredibly bad. This must be the mystification that has led to belief in those diaphanous damsels, the muses of uncertain promise who may, at their capricious wills, hover unseen above the struggling artist, give winged words to the poet and a golden pen to the grateful designer. And at other times the fickle ladies seem to have lost your address altogether.

If one may not dare to describe the gifts of creative workmanship, it should nevertheless be possible to state some of the principles that enter into the planning and production of a well-made book. First of all, the typographer should approach his task with the respectful commitment that the book is a cultural heritage. He or she should be knowledgeable in the origins and development of the alphabet and of type—those twenty-six wonderful letter forms, large and small—that are the substance with which the designer must fashion his book. The book designer should have paid homage to the ancient glory of the illuminated manuscript and have studied the great printed book through its five hundred years. Knowledge of paper and its uses is essential, as is acquaintance with the mechanics and potentialities of printing and binding. These strictures may be occupational platitudes, but they are ignored at one's risk.

The text controls the typographic scheme—or it should—with certain vagaries occasionally to be met. One or two possible examples may illustrate the unexpected problems that can arise. For example, type flows more smoothly in Latin than in English because of the preponderance in Latin of the characters m, n, u, and other letters of equal x height, and the infrequency of b, d, p, and other ascending and descending letters. German, with its capitalization of all nouns, gives the printed page a spotted look. Then there is the Old Testament, which one may be surprised to find is composed largely of one-syllable words in rhythmic and poetic repetition. This permits the use of large type in a narrow measure (short lines of type) without hyphenation. The New Testament, on the other hand, contains a more normal percentage of longer words. Inventive compromise is frequently an unexpected responsibility for the designer that will often force a surprisingly felicitous solution.

The text page, or type page as it is known in the trade, is the heart of the book from which all else radiates. It is the most subtle and most elusive phase in the planning. The designer must be alert to the fact that the final arrangement of the page will be repeated several hundred or perhaps a thousand times, depending on the length of the book. Any lack of harmonious interrelation, every eccentricity, will be repeated without mercy, again and again and again. To the uninitiated, the type page must appear as a rather simple problem. When successful, it will appear logical, easy to read and inevitable, as though no other solution were possible.

The reader may be surprised to learn that Bruce Rogers spent up to a year planning the pages of his great Oxford Lectern Bible, which was four years in production. He said that he wished to avoid a heavy and monumental look. In his own words: "I wanted this book to appear as though I were accustomed to knocking off large folios daily, or at least weekly, as mere routine work." With type alone, without illustration or decoration, Rogers achieved a rare and wonderful combination of clarity, dramatic simplicity, and nobility. Without fear of contradiction one may call his Oxford Bible the greatest printed book of the twentieth century, secure in the company of the noble books of all time.

Clarity, beauty, nobility are the quintessential goals. The first duty of the book designer is to transmit the author's text to the reader without hindrance. Illustration and decoration may well enhance the pages, but the successful arrangement of type is the vital, central concern. That this can be done with imagination and artistry may be seen in the books of the masters, old and new.

The hidden and most subtle factor in the achievement of fine letterpress printing (and the pleasure it can give) is the fineness or quality of the final printed page and the delicate relation of type to paper. This is not easy. When my first book, *Primitives*, was on press, Max Weber, who had cut the wood blocks and was standing by, said, "Let the paper breathe." This simple maxim became an absolute rule at the Spiral Press for a single line of type or for a full page with illustration. Most pressmen tend to overink printed matter. That is the easy way, but the effect is dense or heavy, and if inspected with a magnifying glass, the edges of the type are not sharp. The goal should be maximum coverage with minimum ink, thus with sensitive impression achieving clean, crisp type. To the naked eye the type should be well covered, but a magnifying glass would show the textured paper minutely breaking through the inking. The white paper thereby breathes and gives the page a sense of (invisible) luminosity. This is the core of craftsmanship and the mystery of its gratification. Ben Shahn said in one of his lectures that craftsmanship is a human communication. How true!

PRINTING EDUCATION

After two years with a hand press on a hilltop, the way back to the sidewalks of New York was made easier by a proposal in 1933 from the New School for Social Research that I give a course on book design and production—an addition to their already active arts and crafts groups. Rather than lectures and blackboard instruction, I offered to bring a hand press and organize a workshop course where students could set and print their own pages. There would be two sessions each week at night, two-and-a-half hours each. Thus I became a teacher, one more small and temporary source in the scattered education available to people who wanted direct exposure to the craft. An interesting group of mature students signed up. They all wanted "to get their hands on type." In addition to the expected production people from publishing houses, there were editors, librarians, book illustrators, a bookseller, and a manufacturer of household lamps. Each student was required to plan and design and produce a project with a title page and a few text pages incorporating the bare bones of bookmaking. The completed pieces, which showed considerable imagination, were acquired by the New York Public

Library, whose Curator of Rare Books was a member of the class.

The basic fundamentals of our craft must be mastered, whether or not a student will one day operate an electric computer or a vast offset press. I suggest that every aspiring student set a modicum of type by hand and print his carefully planned pages on a fine sheet of paper on a hand press. These are the basics which provide surprising rewards. And one more absolute—study and enjoy the great books of the masters, designed and printed during five centuries down to our own. They are available to the inquiring mind in all major libraries. These are the ends we sought in the workshop at the New School and in the working courses provided for more than twenty years by the American Institute of Graphic Arts in New York.

All the small fine printing houses have been hospitable to young people who asked for the opportunity to learn and to grow. However, we should especially recall the Rudge and Grabhorn presses as the most productive seedbeds. Among the Rudge alumni, already encountered in these pages, were the designer-proprietors of the Harbor, Peter Pauper, Hawthorn House, and Spiral presses, and several designers and production heads in prominent publishing houses. From the Grabhorns in California came printers Helen Gentry, Gregg Anderson, Sherwood Grover, Andrew Hoyem, and others. At the Spiral Press, Ronald Gordon served two years before he established his own excellent Oliphant Press in New York; Charles Heckscher spent some summer vacation weeks with us; and Leonard Schlosser, later President of the Lindenmeyr Paper Corporation, acknowledges that he discovered the subtleties of presswork during extended visits as a young paper salesman.

At the turn of the century in New England, a well-attended series of lectures was given at the Boston Public Library. In Chicago, Frederic W. Goudy, America's prolific type designer, taught lettering at the Frank Holme School of Illustration. His infectious love of letters brushed off on two future successful type designers—Oswald Cooper and W. A. Dwiggins. Goudy taught lettering from 1916 to

1924 at the Art Students League in New York, as did Howard Trafton a few years later.

From Daniel Berkeley Updike's lectures, delivered from 1911 to 1916 at Harvard University in the Graduate School of Business Administration, came his monumental two-volume classic, *Printing Types: Their History, Forms, and Use.* It was published in 1922 by the Harvard University Press, reprinted several times, and is still available at this writing. And at the Harvard Widener Library, George Parker Winship, "who had a singular genius for infecting undergraduates with a love of books and printing," gave a course, Fine Arts 5e, History of the Printed Book.

Robert W. Nelson, the enlightened president of the American Type Founders Company, provided corporate funds for Henry Lewis Bullen, a dedicated librarian and devotee of printing, to build a typographic library that eventually consisted of some 46,000 historical and contemporary items of prime importance. It was housed in its own ample quarters at the main office of the Company in Elizabeth, New Jersey. The library (where I spent a month of youthful days) was begun in 1908. After many useful years, and after Nelson's death, the A.T.F. Board of Directors withdrew further support from the "unprofitable" unit. In 1936 the collection was moved to Columbia University on deposit, where in 1941 it was finally purchased and permanently housed.

The Carnegie Institute of Technology in Pittsburgh invited Porter Garnett, a knowledgeable California printer with a literary background, to organize and teach a working course devoted to craft within its business-oriented Department of Printing, itself a part of the Institute's College of Industries. Whereupon Garnett set up the Laboratory Press in 1922 with type and hand presses and proceeded to instill in his students his own reverence for the printed book and a thorough grounding in the details of design and production. The Laboratory Press printed and sometimes published until Garnett's retirement in 1935.

Instruction in the Middle West owes much to Carroll Coleman. In 1935, as an instructor in English at the University of Iowa, he set up his Prairie Press and began his distinguished career, printing and publishing the work of contemporary American writers, many of them then unknown. In 1945 he was asked to establish the Typographic Laboratory at Iowa, where he introduced promising students to the art and mystery of type and presses until 1956, when he induced Harry Duncan of the Cummington Press to leave Massachusetts. Duncan took over at Iowa and remained for sixteen years. His beneficent influence has been described by one of his students, K. K. Merker, in a few sentences that also explain why some poets become printers. "Since the University of Iowa was the first in the country to establish a graduate degree in creative writing, Harry's presence at Iowa, with all of his talents, brought a major and spectacular reaction in the writing community. Many writers from the Writers' Workshop became his friends and took his course and, since not all people who want to be Great American Writers can actually make the grade, a number of them, myself included, found that printing was a beguiling substitute. Some used it as a kind of therapy, and others discovered it was their true vocation. Regardless, after Harry's coming, dozens of small presses popped up, most of which disappeared as the proprietors found other interests or careers that were of more importance to them. But some remained and have done important work over the years."

Merker was one who remained. He succeeded his mentor when Duncan moved to the University of Nebraska at Omaha in 1972. There Duncan has again led newcomers into the intriguing ways of hand composition and printing and holds seminars in the history of the printed book. Abbatoir Editions is the imprint for the books produced by Duncan and his students. Subsequently, Merker put together his own private Stone Wall Press in Iowa City, and for the University of Iowa, the Windhover Press of which he is currently the director. Windhover, well equipped and with an excellent assortment of typefaces, is the college typographic workshop.

The University of Wisconsin currently offers typography and printing in its art department with Professor Walter Hamady. Poet and photographer, graduate of Wayne University and the Cranbrook Academy of Art, Hamady prints and publishes books and makes his own excellent paper at his Perishable Press Limited. He named the Press, he said, "to reflect the human conditions, both perishable and limited." He is a highly original manipulator of type and an exceptionally able and innovative pressman. He has inspired a number of his students to pursue typographic careers.

Ray Nash, Professor in the Art Department of Dartmouth College, conducted a very successful workshop from 1937 to 1970 in the art and history of the book. He had been a newspaperman, lecturer in bibliography at Oxford University, and associate at the Plantin-Moretus Museum of Printing in Belgium. His enlightened instruction could be seen in the students he attracted and in their later contributions to the craft. Nash graduates include Roderick Stinehour, printer; David R. Godine, publisher; Alvin Eisenman, Professor in the Yale School of Art; Sinclair Hitchings, Curator at the Boston Public Library; Edward Connery Lathem, Dean of Libraries at Dartmouth; and others.

Victor Hammer was one of the many Hitler refugees who enriched their country of adoption. An eminent painter, type designer, and printer, Hammer arrived in 1939 at Wells College in Aurora, New York. He promptly established the Wells College Press and offered instruction to a few young women who helped with production. In 1948 he accepted the appointment of artist-in-residence at Transylvania College in Lexington, Kentucky, where he again set up his own private press, the Stamperia del Santuccio, in his home. His beautiful printed books, lectures, and writings were the inspiration that made Lexington a nucleus of lively typographic activity. His wife and colleague, Carolyn Reading Hammer, then librarian of the University of Kentucky, in 1956 established the university's

78

King Library Press "as a publishing and teaching institution." This goal was and is still being realized. There is a workshop with four Washington hand presses and accompanying equipment. W. Gay Reading is currently its full-time director. Apprentices come chiefly from the library staff and from the College of Library Science. In addition, three-day seminars on pertinent typographic subjects are held that have drawn speakers and students from two continents.

For thirty years, from 1919 to 1948, Carl Purington Rollins, Printer to Yale University and lecturer, endowed his post with erudition and typographic distinction. Now in the nineteen-eighties, the esthetics of printing are pursued at Yale in the Rollins spirit. In the Art School, Alvin Eisenman is Director of Studies in Graphic Design, primarily for graduate students looking toward professional careers. A lecture and workshop course for undergraduates, Art of the Book, is given by Howard I. Gralla. This course uses the facilities of the Pierson College Press, one of the many colleges at Yale with type and presses available for students' avocational activities. A seminar for graduate students in printing processes is conducted by Greer Allen, University Printer. Substantial backup for these activities is provided by the Yale Library's Arts of the Book collection with Gay Walker, its present devoted curator.

In 1948 the American Institute of Graphic Arts acted on my proposal to establish and sustain a workshop in New York with type and equipment that would enable students to plan and produce their own projects under instruction from our best professional designers and printers. Fortunately, we were able to interest the Board of Education, and the workshop was given space and privileges in the large and extremely well-equipped building that housed their New York School of Printing. Our workshop director was James Hendrickson, a free-lance designer who had been Bruce Rogers' compositor at the Rudge plant and who, for a few years, had been in charge of production for publisher Alfred A. Knopf. A two-year course was offered with the workshop open two nights each week for

79

thirty weeks. As usual with adult education, classes were large (almost 100 students) at the opening of each new session, then dwindled away to less than half as the year made other demands on students' time, energy, and inclinations. Nevertheless, over the more than twenty years that the workshop functioned, a thousand students had registered. They came from publishing houses, foundations, and other organizations concerned with books and printing, and included artists and graphic designers who wanted the feel of type and printing in their own hands. When they left, carrying off their own pages, they had found greater understanding of what was still the heart and soul, if not the hard body, of the new complex technology.

The School of Printing at Rochester Institute of Technology is the largest and best-equipped printing school in the United States. There are 800 undergraduate students who, during a four-year course, work toward a B.S. degree, and fifty graduate students who are candidates for the M.S. degree. Instruction is provided in all phases and techniques of modern printing production, including, of course, computerized processes. The vast percentage of the student body is interested only in those aspects of printing production that lead to commercial management and business success. For the intellectually curious few who wish to discover historical origins and who seek personal expression through exercise of their craft, the Institute provides instruction in the history of the printed book, typographic design, papermaking, bookbinding, etc.

In 1969 the Melbert B. Cary, Jr., Graphic Arts Collection was presented to the Rochester Institute of Technology by the Trustees of the Mary Flagler Cary Charitable Trust with funds for its upkeep and growth. The Collection, presently approaching ten thousand items, with examples from the fine presses of the past and the present, is available to students and the public. The current Cary Professor of Graphic Arts is Herbert H. Johnson, a former student, who has succeeded to the post first held by the highly regarded Alexander S. Lawson. Hermann Zapf, perhaps the most accomplished living pro-

80

fessional calligrapher and type designer, was the second Cary professor and continues as a visiting lecturer. In addition to instruction in calligraphy and classical letter design, he gives students the benefit of his involvement with the problems to be met in the transition from metal type to the new computerized technology.

I must emphasize that this reporting is limited by my own experience. Instruction unfamiliar to me has been provided in New York by New York University, the Book Arts Center, the School of Visual Arts, and others here and throughout the country, especially on the active West Coast.

In his Inaugural Address on the fourth of March, 1933, Franklin Delano Roosevelt promised a depressed and frightened people that "this great nation will endure as it has endured, will revive and prosper. So, first of all, let me assert my firm belief that the only thing we have to fear is fear itself." The promise was kept. By the mid-thirties improvement in the economy was clearly forward; the approach of a second world war in the late thirties made it jump.

After two years of teaching and free-lance designing, I brought together equipment and staff in New York, and late in 1935, wheels were again turning at the Spiral Press. Earlier relationships were quickly renewed and, in fact, the thirties proved to be very productive years for us. In addition to the usual catalogues, bookplates, invitations, stationery, and other ephemera, there were books of verse by W. H. Auden and A. E. Coppard for Random House; two books by Robert Frost for his publishers; our first books for the Limited Editions Club; beginnings with both the Metropolitan Museum of Art and the Museum of Modern Art; and a book program of our own in American literature that we published over the imprint of Rockland Editions.

THE MUSEUM OF MODERN ART

Beginning in the mid-thirties and for the next five or six years, I designed and printed the exhibition catalogues, most of the invitations, and much other ephemera for the Museum of Modern Art. The Museum was founded in 1929. For a few years they occupied a floor in the Heckscher Building at Fifth Avenue and Fifty-seventh Street in New York where the early exhibitions were held. In 1932 they moved into their fine new building on Fifty-third Street and began a very active period with several exhibitions every year. Catalogues varied from 24 pages paperback to 200 pages clothbound. Editions varied from two thousand to five thousand copies. The composition was completed at the Spiral Press for all catalogues, as was the printing except for the large catalogues that were produced under my direct supervision at a neighboring plant. A very few typical titles among very many, of exhibitions and their catalogues, would include work by Vincent van Gogh, Georges Rouault, Frank Lloyd Wright, Charles Sheeler, John Marin, Walker Evans; and group shows, such as Cubism and Abstract Art, Photography 1839–1937, New Horizons in American Art, Masters of Popular Painting, Modern Architecture in England, Fantastic Art, Dada, Surrealism, the Bauhaus.

Texts were set by Linotype or Monotype with hand makeup. Printing was letterpress on dull-coated paper. For invitations during those years when membership lists were comparatively small, we could frequently use interesting imported papers. If one may look back a half century, the thirties are now seen as a considerably smaller and much easier period, less emotional and less violent. Those Museum catalogues were typical, I believe, of agreeable personal and working relationships. As the deadline neared for an exhibition opening, with type set and plates made for the catalogue, I would go to the Museum by appointment usually late in the afternoon. The two young women responsible for editorial work and production, respectively Ernestine Fantl and Frances Collins, and Alfred H. Barr, director of the institution, who had written the text, would gather around a table with scissors and pastepots, and there we would put together a set of page proofs. Sandwiches and coffee came along in due course, and by ten o'clock the catalogue had taken final form. This, with some affection, was called the "diddle-and-paste" session, after which the streets of New York were then safe enough to allow the printer to walk or ride home with the OK secure in his briefcase. I cannot imagine that a director of today's museums with their manifold responsibilities could engage in a serious encounter with a pastepot.

As the Museum enlarged in scope, with its vastly greater audience, its printing needs grew beyond the capacities of a small fine shop. However, a dozen years later, in 1952, I was invited to produce an edition of *Twelve Fables of Aesop*, newly narrated by Glenway Wescott and illustrated by Antonio Frasconi. Its colophon tells the story: "This book, the first of a series of limited editions to be published by The Museum of Modern Art under the direction of Monroe Wheeler, has been designed and printed by Joseph Blumenthal at The Spiral Press, New York on Rives mould-made paper. The Emerson type has been set by hand, and the illustrations have been separately printed from the artist's original blocks. The edition is limited to 975 numbered copies and 25 lettered review copies, all signed by Mr. Frasconi, Mr. Wescott and Mr. Blumenthal."

A second book in the series appeared in 1957— *Voyages, Six Poems* by Hart Crane, with superb wood engravings by Leonard Baskin, designed and handsomely printed by Baskin at his Gehenna Press in Northampton, Massachusetts. With the *Aesop* and *Voyages* a very promising enterprise came to an untimely and regrettable end.

THE PUBLIC PAPERS AND ADDRESSES
OF FRANKLIN D. ROOSEVELT

One day in 1936 a telephone call from Donald Klopfer of Random House began a memorable experience. He and Bennett Cerf had been approached by Judge Samuel I. Rosenman concerning possible publication of the Roosevelt public addresses and state papers. Rosenman, who had been legal counsel to Roosevelt as Governor of New York, and later as President of the United States, would be the coordinator and editor of the final publication.

Roosevelt wanted to see his history-making words in book form during his own lifetime, with an introduction to be written by him for each volume, and with notes to describe the origins of each of the major documents and the circumstances that called for their delivery. There were to be five volumes—one for the governorship, 1928–1932, and one for each of the presidential years, 1933, 1934, 1935, and 1936. Included would be the inaugural addresses, messages to Congress, press conferences, the popular "fireside" chats, and a host of other pertinent documents.

Judge Rosenman asked Random House and two or three other houses to submit proposals for publication and to show rather comprehensive proofs of text and title pages and bindings. My job was to prepare this material for competition with the other publishers. The central typographic problems involved the need to fuse the papers and addresses with the notes and to give many kinds of data a sense of homogeneity in clear, readable, easily recognized and assimilable form. The books were to reflect the importance of the subject matter, but to be neither ostentatious nor forbidding. We settled on a page 6½ x 9½ inches. The papers and addresses were set in 12-point Linotype Baskerville, full measure; the subsidiary notes, to set them apart, in 10-point, double column. Mr. Roosevelt was a sophisticated collector, a buyer of press books, and an Honorary Member of the Grolier Club from 1934 until his death. He was therefore more than ordinarily concerned with the physical appearance of this, his monument in print. Once the various proposals had been submitted, Mr. Roosevelt's decision was quickly made. Random House was chosen as publisher, and my typographic arrangement was accepted without change.

Specimen text pages, title pages, and other special details were then set and proofed at the Spiral Press. From these as guides, the composition of the 3600 pages and the final printing and binding were done at the Haddon Craftsmen in Camden, New Jersey. I supervised production all the way.

Presidential papers had normally been issued in small editions at high prices, purchased by libraries and a few historians. Because of the importance of the Roosevelt period and because of the introductions and notes especially written for these volumes, a wide reader appeal was anticipated provided the books could be issued at attractively low prices. Cerf and Klopfer therefore decided to print 8000 copies of each volume at $3.00 per copy, $15.00 for the five volumes boxed. But the books did not meet the expected reception from the book-buying public, perhaps because they appeared right after the Supreme Court "packing" controversy when Roosevelt's popularity was at a low ebb. In any event a substantial percentage of the edition was remaindered. After a few years they were hard to find. The eight volumes subsequent to the 1936 presidential year were issued by other publishing houses in small and high-priced editions.

There seem to be no records available of the course of the books' production. It may be dangerous to depend on one's memory forty-five years after the event, but I recall vividly the speed and care that Roosevelt gave to every detail in these five volumes. The notes had been prepared by Rosenman and by Cabinet members or other officials originally involved. Mr. Roosevelt made very extensive galley corrections. Unless my memory deceives me, these author's alterations came to eight thousand dollars and they were paid by the President's personal check. But these galley proofs cannot be found

85

at the Hyde Park Library. We did find the original typed pages at the Library of the five introductions with Mr. Roosevelt's handwritten corrections (they were shown at the Spiral Press exhibition at the Morgan Library), but the galleys of the main text have never turned up. I also recall that as each batch of proofs went to Judge Rosenman and then to the White House, they were always returned in about five days, read and corrected by Mr. Roosevelt whether he was in Washington or on his campaign train during the 1936 election. A letter from Donald Klopfer to me, dated 15 July 1980, confirms in general his recall of the events here put down. His letter concludes: ". . . but I don't believe any of that material was kept. We were never smart enough to think that we were publishing for posterity."

Finally completed, the books apparently met with the President's approval. A set was signed for me on the title page of Volume One: "To Joseph Blumenthal, A-1 Designer, from his friend, Franklin D. Roosevelt, 1938."

THE TYPOPHILES

Informal Wednesday luncheons in New York during the early thirties grew into a loose but highly productive organization of professionals who called themselves the Typophiles. Over the years they combined gustatory conviviality and devotion to craft with the preparation, printing, and publishing of significant books that have become scholarly, historical records of a fertile period. Printers, graphic artists, paper manufacturers, bookbinders, librarians, and others involved in the world of type, who took pleasure in their work and who enjoyed a refreshing spirit of camaraderie, were held together by the lighthearted and inspiring leadership of Paul A. Bennett of the Mergenthaler Linotype Company. He was, I believe, the typographic conscience of our generation. There were no officers and no dues; Paul was the omniscient and benevolent high priest.

86

Printed keepsakes at dinners for our elders and betters soon grew into a series of interesting Chap Books. The pattern was first set in 1935 at an evening gathering to celebrate the seventieth birthday of Fred Goudy. A few dozen friends and admirers wrote and printed pieces about Goudy, his devoted typesetting wife, and about his many typefaces. The signatures were bound together and titled *Spinach From Many Gardens*, with several copies "fed" to the guest of honor and a copy for each diner. A few months later Bruce Rogers returned from England after four years during which, among other memorable books, he had designed and supervised production of his Oxford Lectern Bible. That epic achievement, and his return to our midst, called for celebration and a festive gathering. *Barnacles From Many Bottoms* was the Chap Book "scraped together" for the man who loved sailing, by seven who drew, fifteen who wrote, and twenty-six who printed—all of it orchestrated by Paul Bennett. These small editions overnight became the despair of collectors.

More group projects followed as freely offered participation became contagious. Bennett called on the leading practitioners of his generation; they responded with enthusiasm to his love of books and printing, and gave their best. In 1936 the indispensable ampersand, often modest, sometimes flamboyant, was pursued and portrayed by thirty-five contributors, including a poem printed on ampersand-paper. Next came a fat little volume called *The Typophiles Left to Their Own Devices*, with 156 different versions of the letter "T," some quite simple, some overladen. Each device was reproduced with an accompanying descriptive note by the designer. And so it went through more than fifty titles during the next thirty years, with a format that became standardized at 4½ x 7 inches. The subject matter became more serious and more scholarly, with greater emphasis on contemporary work. Happily, the circle of contributors grew to include men and women from the American West and colleagues in Europe.

The Chap Books began to reflect our awareness that we were in the presence of men of stature whose achievements we were privileged to record. A sampling of titles should be of interest. Biographies (a few from the past) and monographs—some in pamphlets, some in two bound volumes with reproductions—were concerned with Thomas Bewick, John Baskerville, Eric Gill, Stanley Morison, Jan van Krimpen, Hermann Zapf, and others from abroad; the Americans included Theodore Low De Vinne, Will Bradley, Frederic W. Goudy, Bruce Rogers, W. A. Dwiggins, Carl Purington Rollins, Lawrence C. Wroth, Alfred A. Knopf, John Howard Benson, Elmer Adler. Typical general titles touched English private presses, roman numerals, calligraphy, early American currency, book publishing, and even a learned disquisition on the venerable composing stick.

The inquiring reader of these notes may wonder at a hit-and-miss program. In a diverse group of individuals an idea would be pursued and occasionally accepted. Then it was necessary for Paul Bennett to find writers, designers, printers, and binders who would undertake projects that he called adventures in enthusiasm. Often they took many years. None would have been accepted by a commercial publisher. There was a subscription list that paid for cash expenditures, and whenever a title showed promise of some ready bookstore sales, extra copies were printed. Paper was usually contributed. Bookkeeping, such as it was, and shipping were accomplished by Bennett and friends he would "invite" to his home for an evening to pack and label and mail.

Perhaps I should add that I participated with printed pieces for all the many group projects, and was also designer and printer of four complete editions. They were *On Conjugal Felicity* (1941), *B.R. Marks & Remarks* (1946), *Woodcuts by Antonio Frasconi* (1957), and *Recalling Peter: The Life and Times of Peter Beilenson and His Peter Pauper Press* (1964).

The Typophiles have survived into the eighties led by Robert L. "Doc" Leslie and Abe Lerner. The faces are new, and the membership is larger and more diffuse than the group of practitioners who first met in the thirties. Gone too are the printing houses with their readily available automatic letterpress equipment. But the spirit of inquiry and devotion to fine printing remains, with monthly meetings and the publication of pertinent Chap Books. An offshoot has appeared in New England. Under the leadership of typographic designer Eugene Ettenburg, "Typophiles in the Country" meet once each month except when winter snows block the roads.

PRINTER AS PUBLISHER

Excursions into publishing have always seemed the best use of the idle hours that occur inevitably in every printing shop. But beyond its practicality, the temptation to make books of one's own choice under one's own control is challenging and compelling. I doubt that any of the printers mentioned in these pages have escaped the lure of type and presses readily at hand, and the seductive gamble of publishing. A few printers, notably the Grabhorns in San Francisco and the Beilensons at their Walpole Printing Office/Peter Pauper Press in the East, devoted themselves primarily to their own publications, but also welcomed suitable printing commissions. At the Spiral Press our infrequently published books, which were enjoyable extracurricular projects, always gave way to printing for others.

My first book, *Primitives*, already described, was followed in 1927 by *Phillida and Coridon*, a slender collection of pastoral lyrics by the Elizabethan poet Nicholas Breton, which I edited and for which I wrote a brief introduction. The altogether charming illustrations by the young painter Ernest Fiene were printed from photoengraved lineplates of pen-and-ink drawings, with colors printed directly from linoleum blocks. The edition was 425 copies. The delicate type, hand-set, designed by Rudolf Koch, was later imported by the Continental Typefounders Company and called "Eve."

Believing that unavailable and unusual titles in American litera-

89

ture would be a sound basis for an interesting program of well-made books, I enlisted the generous help of scholars in the field. In 1929 we issued *The Day of Doom* by Michael Wigglesworth, a seventeenth-century New England divine. This was a Calvinistic tract in the form of a fire-and-brimstone narrative poem that was a bestseller in colonial America. The text was edited and introduced by Professor Kenneth B. Murdock of Harvard University, and Wanda Gág made very appropriate drawings with motifs taken from New England gravestones. The type was machine-set Intertype Garamond. *The Day of Doom* has since been issued by a reprint house, reproduced from our edition. More than fifty years since our date of publication, I still receive a small royalty check twice each year.

During 1929 we also completed the *Poems of Edgar Allan Poe*, which I chose because I thought Poe's long lines should be read unbroken, not turned-over. To my knowledge they had not before been so printed. The book was edited, with an introduction, by Professor Howard Mumford Jones, then at the University of North Carolina. It was hand-set in Lutetia type and machine-printed on a lovely French handmade paper in generous format. A knowledge-able friend, Abe Lerner, recently identified the paper by the water-mark of a female nude, and an "M" within a circle, to have been made by sculptor Maillol's nephew, who made similar paper for the great Cranach Presse books. Bennett Cerf thought well enough of our books to offer Random House distribution. However, the De-pression was just around the corner and this program, with some promising books in prospect, was, like so many others, put aside.

After the Depression I assumed that scarce and desirable material in American literature could be well designed and printed on fine paper in limited editions, and find a market at prices considerably above the level of mass-produced trade books. With more optimism than good judgment, I established Rockland Editions, our own im-print. I again approached Professor Jones, who had moved to Har-vard, and as always, scholars responded with enthusiasm. A committee suggested a number of interesting titles, including the work of a hitherto unknown colonial poet and a volume on the American comic legend.

Thomas H. Johnson, well-known scholar in American literature, had discovered a 400-page manuscript in the Yale University Library containing the poems of Edward Taylor. An orthodox Puritan minister, Taylor lived nearly sixty years in the frontier village of Westfield, Massachusetts, and wrote poetry until 1725 "in the mannered style of the pre-Restoration sacred poets — and in the tradition of Donne and the Anglo-Catholic conceitists." Greeted favorably by academic scholars, our publication, *The Poetical Works of Edward Taylor*, was the authentic first edition of an important, if minor, American poet. In 1939 we printed 925 copies in Baskerville type.

The second title, *Davy Crockett, American Comic Legend* (1939), was edited by Richard M. Dorson, then a graduate student at Harvard, who later became an authority on American folk literature. The text came from the almanacs that appeared from 1835 to 1856, first in Nashville and then in cities throughout the East from Louisville to Boston. These were the tall tales of the epic American frontier, stories of Indian fighting and pioneer heroes, fantastic adventures of legendary characters. In a review in the *New York Herald Tribune*, Lewis Gannett called these tales the American *Iliad* and *Niebelungenlied*. Included in our edition were faithful reproductions of the crude but vivacious woodcuts that illustrated the stories in the decades before the Civil War. The edition was 925 copies in Bookman type with Ultra-Bodoni headings.

Despite considerable sales efforts these books were substantial losses both in time and money. The costs in time were especially burdensome and I learned that publishing must be a major effort, or, better, left to the professionals. Printers had better stick to their type and watch their p's and q's. Rockland Editions died aborning, but both published books were worth the work, and I believe that both editors agreed. Unsold copies of the Edward Taylor were bought and republished by Princeton University Press, and *Davy Crockett* was acquired and sold out by E. Weyhe, the New York bookseller and art dealer.

Two of my favorite books were made with Ben Shahn. *The Alphabet of Creation* is one of the legends from the *Sefer Ha-Zohar*, or *Book of Splendor*, an ancient Gnostic work written in Aramaic by a thirteenth-century Spanish scholar, Moses de Leon, who presented the work, not as his own, but as mystic knowledge revealed many centuries earlier. Our edition was adapted by Shahn from the English translation by Maurice Samuel. The legend relates how each letter of the alphabet descends from the crown of God and entreats that the world be created through it. Shahn's superb pen-and-ink drawings included his very personal versions of the twenty-two letters of the Hebrew alphabet, which we printed from photoengraved line plates. Fifty copies set in 24-point Emerson type on Umbria handmade paper we issued ourselves, and 500 copies on mouldmade Rives paper from France were purchased for publication by Kurt Wolff of Pantheon Books. Two popular offset editions, reproduced from our printing, were later published: in cloth by Knopf at five dollars per copy, and paperbound by Schocken at one dollar each. I recall having luncheon with a friend at Lindy's popular restaurant on Broadway when *The Alphabet of Creation* was on press. I told him the story, unaware that I was overheard by our waiter standing behind me. When I finished he tapped me on the shoulder and said, "Mister, that ain't a new story, my grandmother told it to me when I was a kid."

Inasmuch as Shahn and I were thwarted in our anticipation of together completing an edition of *The Living Talmud* for the Limited Editions Club, I suggested Ecclesiastes in the King James Version of the Bible, which we would print and publish ourselves at the Spiral Press. Ben agreed with fervor and made three marvelous drawings that evoked the grandeur of the ancient Hebrew prophets. They were engraved by Shahn's young neighbor, Stefan Martin, on wood that we printed directly from the blocks. David Soshensky added a calligraphic page and made a new paragraph mark that we had cut in metal solely for this publication. Hand-set in 18-point Emerson type, page size 9½ x 13 inches, an edition of 285 copies was bound in vellum and buckram over boards. It sold easily at the considerable price in 1965 of fifty dollars per copy.

PRINTING HOUSES
AND THE ARTISTS

The human need to embellish was well served from the 1890's to mid-century by the many fortunate relationships that existed between the small printing houses and those artists and designers whose aptitudes and inclinations led them to the printed book. Among such alliances the most conspicuous examples were Bertram Grosvenor Goodhue and Rudolph Ruzicka with Updike in Boston; Will Bradley and Frederic W. Goudy at their own presses; Bruce Rogers and Frederic Warde at Rudge; Rockwell Kent, Lucien Bernhard, and T. M. Cleland at Adler's Pynson Printers; Valenti Angelo and Mallette Dean at the Grabhorn Press; W. A. Dwiggins and Warren Chappell with publisher Knopf; Joseph Low, Victor Hammer, and Leonard Baskin, painters who operated their own presses; and the many illustrators whose work enhanced the books of the Peter Pauper Press. No listing, however incomplete, should omit mention of the books that were printed at the private Overbrook and Allen presses, nor the many artists in many countries who responded to George Macy's invitations to illustrate for the Limited Editions Club. Picasso and Matisse said yes to Macy, as did nearer home, Grant Wood, John Steuart Curry, and numerous others.

A phenomenon not to be overlooked was the burst of new book types that accompanied the printing house-artist relationships. Recapitulation of the surprising number of designers of such typefaces would include Goodhue, Ruzicka, Bradley, Goudy, Rogers,

93

Warde, Cleland, Bernhard, Dwiggins, Chappell, Hammer—and among others, your present reporter. Of the completed types, some were private faces; most were made on order from commercial foundries and widely used. If design for metal type is a thing of the past, letter design is not. Several competent designers are struggling with the problems involved in film composition and the computer, now in the first stages of development. That story belongs to some future historian.

Some of America's most respected artists added luster to work turned out at the Spiral Press. During our first years we sent calendars to friends and customers with woodcuts made for us by young American printmakers whose work I saw in New York's art galleries. In 1927 and 1928 Howard Cook and Emil Ganso cut blocks with scenes of New York; in 1929 Wanda Gág made hers of equipment in our shop. These and later working relationships which, to quote Robert Frost, involved "love and need" produced much of our best printed matter—and friendships that lasted a lifetime.

Successful production of a meaningful book brings deep and lasting satisfactions. The experience is greatly enhanced by a fruitful working relationship with the artist if the book is to be illustrated. I believe that the physical conception of the book should start with the typographic designer, who will then show general format, paper, and type arrangement to the illustrator. Reciprocal adjustments, if advisable, should then produce an integrated result.

I recall that when Kurt Wolff asked me to design and print a bestiary to be published by Pantheon Books in a limited edition, the drawings of the many animals had already been completed by Alexander Calder following the typescript by the poet Richard Wilbur, editor and translator. I had never before met Calder, famous for his mobiles. When I asked him if the drawings were preliminary sketches, he reduced me with a look that said they were absolutely final, of course. Nevertheless, I quietly went to work on a large format and set up a few pages in Scotch Roman type with Bulmer for

94

display, with space left for illustration. On a pleasant spring day in Connecticut, I drove to Calder's studio in Roxbury from my home in West Cornwall, proofs in hand. A huge mobile scaled to the surrounding trees stood outside his house. With each of rather many visits he decided to remake his drawings to fit on the pages as he saw them take form depending on the body — length and width of lines — of the different poems. An additional bonus might be a light luncheon in his home, which was full of delectable ashtrays, jewelry, kitchen utensils, and other bizarre concoctions he had made of wire. (His wife, Louisa, is a niece of Henry James.) His huge studio in a separate building was a jumbled wonderland of mobiles and stabiles. Eventually he made new pen-and-ink drawings for every one of the more than seventy pages. The solid line drawings reproduced faithfully when printed from photoengraved lineplates. A Calder bear hug at the end of the summer and a good book in late autumn were among the prizes in a friendly duel between book designer and artist. Both parties won.

Ben Shahn was one of the few prominent American artists who did not retreat to the painter's ivory tower. With a strong social sense and a highly articulate pen, he cut a wide swath in the life and art of his time. We first met when we were both on a jury for the American Institute of Graphic Arts to select work submitted for a large exhibition, "Printing for Commerce." Shahn was shocked at the lush extravagance of the printed matter in contrast to its lack of originality and good taste. We agreed as jurors and thus began a long friendship and productive working relationship.

Shahn approached a promotional piece of printing for the Columbia Broadcasting System or a portrait cover for *Time* magazine with the same application to purpose that he gave to a painting on canvas. His first drawings as a child in Russia were the letters of the Hebrew alphabet. This was love at first sight, and the infinite variety never withered. Later, in the United States he became a lithographer's apprentice at age fourteen when, in his own words, "I discovered the Roman alphabet in all its elegance and its austere dignity, and I fell in love all over again with letters. To make a perfect Roman letter . . . I suppose I spent months just on the A alone." Late in life Shahn celebrated this long devotion in a splendid book appropriately called *Love and Joy About Letters*, published in 1963, which reproduced in color his many paintings and prints in which his lettering—sometimes a complete Psalm—was an essential part of the picture. He asked his publisher to have the book designed and the text set at the Spiral Press in Emerson, Shahn's "favorite type."

Except for children's books, I object to illustration in which the artist attempts literal portrayal. If we are dealing with significant literature, the allegory, the symbolism, and the vitality should be a direct and private communication between the author and the reader. Illustration can also be subtle and symbolic and can at the same time satisfy the natural desire for decoration. Ideally, illustration should be a work of art that will complement and enhance a worthy text, not be competitive. Shahn agreed, and I believe we succeeded in achieving these desirable ends in *The Alphabet of Creation* and in our edition of *Ecclesiastes*—books that grew out of personal enthusiasms.

Artists from Albrecht Dürer to woodcutters and wood engravers of our own time have, with a small knife or graver, transformed plain pieces of wood into works of art. The woodcut is the most ancient, honorable, and natural means of making multiple impressions on paper. It is a simple and direct method with results as different as there are different kinds of wood, paper, and kinds of artists. At the Spiral Press we printed innumerable artists' blocks as separate editions of prints or as illustrations in books. Blocks can be printed by hand in the artist's studio in small editions on a hand press or by rubbing with the back of a spoon or other instrument. Or they can be produced on an automatic printing press in a much larger number of impressions. A printing press is, certainly, a much more complex tool than a spoon. Its function, nevertheless, is the same as that of a spoon—the application of ink to paper via impression. In both methods the depth, textures, and other qualities in the final print will depend entirely on the imagination, skill, and affection with which the tools are manipulated. Grain and texture of the wood and of the paper can be held by both methods, with paper an all-important factor. The high cost of fine papers favors the artist's small edition. Lithography and etching are the other media for artists' prints. All processes were used with great success in the famous French *livres d'artistes*.

Twenty-five years of a fruitful relationship began in the 1940's when Antonio Frasconi brought us a woodcut for the catalogue of his first exhibition in New York. Born in Uruguay of Italian parents, the warmth of the Mediterranean shines in his work, whether black-and-white or in his abundant use of color. Unlike the wood engravers who cut on the smooth grain of hard wood, Frasconi cuts on coarse woods whose grain and texture become an integral part of the final print. His bold cutting invited printing on papers of all kinds and surfaces that added interest to the design—and provided healthy challenge in production to our men on the presses. Over the years we printed invitations and catalogues for his many exhibitions in this country and abroad; also a miscellany that included book and record jackets and specimen settings for books to be issued by his trade publishers.

Two of the books printed at the Spiral Press with Frasconi woodcuts have already been mentioned: *Twelve Fables of Aesop* for the Museum of Modern Art, and *Woodcuts by Antonio Frasconi* issued by the Typophiles. Of the *Woodcuts* there was a special printing published by the Weyhe Gallery in New York of 500 copies on Japanese Goyu handmade paper with an introductory note by the artist and a brief statement by the volume's printer on the printing of woodcuts.

In 1965 Margaret McElderry at Harcourt, Brace & World commissioned a bilingual edition of a bestiary in verse by the famous Chilian poet, Pablo Neruda. Entitled *Bestiary/Bestiario*, the page was

97

an ample 8⅛ x 11⅜ inches, type was 18-point Emerson. The woodcuts in two colors by Frasconi were large and lusty. We printed a limited 300 signed and numbered copies on Rives mouldmade paper and 3500 copies on a domestic sheet for the trade edition. In 1974 a facsimile paperback was published by Harcourt, offset from our original edition.

In close collaboration we printed a few handsome and engaging small books for Antonio on Walt Whitman, Henry David Thoreau, and others, which he planned, wrote, illustrated, and published with success. Long since out of print, these modest volumes are eagerly sought by collectors. It is of real interest to add that Frasconi, who has been extremely skillful in printing his large blocks by hand, is now experimenting with Xerox color "printing" for artist editions of prints on the machine built for inexpensive copies of forms in business offices.

Fritz Eichenberg, one of several artists who brought their conspicuous talents to this country from Nazi Germany, has been a major proponent of wood engraving in the United States. Wood engraving has been a favorite medium for book illustration since Thomas Bewick brought it to a high degree of excellence in the eighteenth century in England where it has had a strong and continuing tradition. Involved is meticulous skill with a graver that cuts the fine white lines on the polished end grain of hardwood, preferably especially prepared Turkish boxwood. Engraved blocks, if printed by letterpress, must be run on very smooth, plated or coated paper to cover the solid black areas that require heavy inking in contrast to the delicately cut shallow lines that require a minimum of ink. For books whose editions normally run to some length, this conflict demands utmost vigilance in press preparation and running. Paradoxically, offset printing can overcome the problem by reproduction from the artist's print instead of direct impression from the block. But that means printing without impression, and that is heresy to the faithful. However, an additional advantage in offset is its ability to print the engravings on a paper with some surface texture, which is best for type, thus avoiding the need for two kinds of paper, or alternatively, printing all on a smooth sheet.

I first met Eichenberg when we were both instructors at the New School for Social Research in New York in the thirties. Our first joint effort was a harmonious combination of type and a wood engraving for one of the pages in a group project organized by Paul Bennett entitled *Peter Piper's Practical Principles of Plain and Perfect Pronunciation* (1936). During the next forty years we printed many of the Eichenberg blocks. Two books came along, commissioned by George Macy for the Limited Editions Club, for which Fritz made woodcut illustrations: Turgenev's *Fathers and Sons* (1951) and Tolstoy's *Resurrection* (1963).

As already mentioned on page 41, I found in Thomas W. Nason (called a pastoral poet on wood) a fine artist and an extraordinary engraver. In addition to the Frost books printed at the Spiral Press and our Christmas cards, Nason made some enchanting vignettes for Frost's *You Come Too* (1959), a trade edition subtitled "Favorite Poems for Young Readers," which I designed for Frost's publisher.

One of the most versatile artists, to whom I frequently and successfully turned for work to be done, was Fritz Kredel, a Hitler refugee whose reputation preceded him and who was warmly welcomed. Formerly a close associate of Rudolf Koch at the famous workshop in Offenbach, Kredel had a magic knife with which he made a lively, vibrant woodcut out of a pedestrian pen-and-ink sketch. One such example was his faithful cutting of the presidential seal for our printing of the Kennedy Inaugural Address of 20 January 1961. This tall but slender volume also included the first printing of Robert Frost's "Dedication for John F. Kennedy, His Inauguration." The few lines that Frost had written for the inaugural ceremony he was unable to read because of the glaring winter sun in his eyes. It is my own private and unsubstantiated opinion that Frost, perhaps subconsciously, welcomed a heaven-sent excuse not

99

to read them. (He was never able to write acceptably to order.) He did speak, extemporaneously, his splendid poem "The Gift Outright." For our printing Frost welcomed the opportunity to expand the unread words into 177 lines, which he playfully called a brief history of the United States. The book was printed in an edition of 500 copies for friends of the Spiral Press and of Frost's publisher, Holt, Rinehart & Winston. President Kennedy signed a copy for me, and shortly thereafter Mrs. Kennedy was interested in having a reprint made for them to send as Christmas gifts to their friends. I submitted two or three elegant dummies with leather bindings, but after several telephone calls from the White House, the idea was abandoned.

I became deeply indebted to Howard Trafton, an artist with a flair for lettering that he taught at the Art Students League of New York during the twenties and thirties. Along with other graphic work, he designed a flowing calligraphic typeface appropriately called Trafton Script, issued by the American Type Founders, which had considerable vogue for some years. I bought a complete range of sizes and used it with pleasure when a decorative touch was needed. In the course of Trafton's preparation of initial letters to enliven the opening pages of our printing of *The Secret* (Fountain Press, 1929), an enchanting slender volume of short stories by A. A. Milne, I must have become too critical. Howard objected and said that if I was so sure how the initials should look, "Why don't you do them yourself?" I protested my lack of skill and lack of tools. Next day an art store delivered a drawing table with pens and drawing instruments. It was a joke—at my expense—because a bill came with the delivery. Howard was right, I discovered that I *could* draw initial letters. Without this tyrannical but benevolent prod, the Emerson type might never have materialized.

Sculptor and printmaker Leonard Baskin is also a highly skilled woodcutter and wood engraver. He engraved some sharp and prickly plants for more than one Spiral Press project. I am pleased to recall his presence among our type cabinets and presses where he must have inhaled some good printer's ink in the years before he established his own Gehenna Press in Northampton, Massachusetts. There he designed and printed charming ephemera for his friends, and large, opulent books of literary consequence for collectors. He closed the Press when he went to live in England in 1975. I wonder what happened to the oriental rug that was on the floor in front of his Kelly press.

Joseph Low, another artist who later set up his own equipment, accepted commissions from the Spiral Press that he would execute in wood or linoleum. At his Eden Hill Press in Newtown, Connecticut, he printed and published his whimsical beasts and people until he sold his press and acquired a boat on which he sailed the Caribbean, invited the wind, and gave no further thought to printing.

One of the annual projects that enabled me to bring artists into our domain was a series of promotional booklets in Americana commissioned by the Curtis Paper Company of Newark, Delaware. This was a small mill whose president, Allen Horton, loved paper and wanted to see wise words and good printing on their interesting product. The design, including the selection of illustrators, was left entirely in my hands. Each June, historian Earl Schenck Miers prepared a text of some thirty-two pages on an unfamiliar aspect of American history that we printed in an edition of 25,000 copies. The paper was usually "Curtis Rag," a successful sheet in the Curtis line-up that was originally made to my specifications. The series started with Thomas Jefferson's first draft of the Declaration of Independence, which included the startling proposal that slavery be abolished in the new United States of America. Alas, Jefferson's draft was rejected in committee. The exceptional talents—calligraphic and illustrative—of Reynard Biemiller, Jeanyee Wong, George Salter, Philip Grushkin, David Soshensky, Stefan Martin, and other artists added lively dimensions to these typographic ventures that continued for some twenty varied years.

Rey Biemiller was my associate at the Spiral Press for fourteen productive years. His calligraphy decorated much of our work, including a few title pages that might otherwise have suffered from rigidity. With good and sufficient reason he finally accepted an invitation to join the Rockefeller University Press in New York, where he designed their books and everything else at that research and teaching institution that called for taste and skill with letter forms written, printed, or cut in metal.

I called on Philip Grushkin for much help. He provided Steuben Glass with their invaluable logo. He made a vigorous calligraphic "75" for the title page of our printing of *Grolier 75* and, among many other assignments, his pen brought forth bright stars and Christmas trees that embellished our Frost cards and other holiday indulgences.

A few artists have so far escaped mention in these pages. Loren MacIver, one of America's most respected painters, made an image on slate of the attenuated soul of the steeplebush plant, which decorated the cover stamped in gold and the title page printed in grey, of Robert Frost's volume of poems in 1947, *Steeple Bush*. Clare Leighton, a noted English wood engraver who came to this country and stayed, brought many of her blocks to be printed. Armin Landeck, American printmaker famous for etchings of city rooftops, made the drawings for the Frost Christmas poem of 1935, *On Making Certain Anything Has Happened*. J. J. Lankes, a popular wood engraver of country scenes, illustrated two of the Frost Christmas poems: *Neither Out Far Nor In Deep* (1935) and *To a Young Wretch* (1937). Warren Chappell, with whom there were many years of professional friendship, brought us the commission from the Limited Editions Club to print Edgar Lee Masters' *Spoon River Anthology* (1942), which Chappell designed and which Boardman Robinson illustrated. Abe Birnbaum, whose work appeared on many *New Yorker* magazine covers, made fine drawings for a Curtis booklet, *The Civil War Letters of W. A. Roebling*, builder of the noble Brooklyn Bridge. Bernard Childs proved me wrong when I told him that his ideas were not feasible for an automatic printing press. He manipulated a type-high copper surface with his power tools, asked for a split fountain to spread the ink, and achieved some extraordinarily ingenious and interesting prints that could be run in any quantity. Michael McCurdy made wood engravings, which we printed from his original blocks, for our production of *The Brick Moon* (1971) for the Imprint Society in Barre, Massachusetts; and for *A Discourse Utter'd in Part at Ammaus-keeg-Falls in the Fishing Season, 1739* (1971) issued by the Barre Publishers of the same city. McCurdy has since established his own Penmaen Press in Lincoln, Massachusetts, where he illustrates and prints and publishes interesting books.

Books that have been vehicles primarily for artists' illustrations such as the famous French *livres d'artistes* are not quite relevant to the present volume but should be noted for the interested student. Museums, libraries, and book clubs have shown the work, much of it spectacular. Two exhibitions were especially noteworthy because comprehensive clothbound catalogues with copious illustrations were published. Work by the most famous painters of the present century who illustrated books were shown in one or both of these exhibitions. "Painters and Sculptors as Illustrators" opened at the Museum of Modern Art in New York in 1936, organized by Monroe Wheeler, who also wrote an illuminating text. "The Artist and the Book" was shown at the Boston Museum of Fine Arts in 1961. The work was chosen by Philip Hofer for the comprehensive volume *The Artist and the Book, 1860–1960, in Western Europe and the United States.*

WORLD WAR II

The 1930's saw the rise of Hitler and, toward the end of the decade, the outbreak of World War II. During 1931, when the Emerson type was in work, it was beyond belief that Hitler would ever take over the German state. As the calamitous decade unfolded in Germany, I signed papers that enabled five Jewish boys to come to the United States. One had been a student in the graphic arts academy in Vienna; another who enlisted in the United States Army became an interrogation officer in the front lines and came out of the war a decorated young major. All fought for their newly adopted country, and all later carried their own weight as citizens.

The attack on Pearl Harbor on 7 December 1941 brought us into the war with Germany as well as with Japan. Inasmuch as the conflict with Hitler had special significance for me, I offered my services as a civilian in the war effort. It appeared that I could be of some use at the Army Map Service in Washington. Therefore in 1942 type and presses were put into storage, and work in process was transferred to the Marchbanks Press, where our customers would be well served for the war's duration. Then my wife and I joined the army of civilians in the nation's capital who crowded into rooming houses and stood in line for meals.

The Army Map Service with several thousand civilian and military personnel in its underground bomb-proof building was a division of the Corps of Engineers responsible for cartography, printing, and distribution of the millions of maps needed in a highly mobile war, fought worldwide on, above, and under the earth. Although the Map Service had its own considerable plant in Washington with sophisticated photographic and offset printing facilities, the demand for maps was so overwhelming, and the time so urgent, that much of the actual printing was contracted to offset printers throughout the country. Assignments were split among contractors in order that military secrecy would be protected.

Because of the need for enormous production and speed, mapping had become mechanized. Whereas before World War I a map was researched, data compiled and drawn by a single knowledgeable and skillful individual requiring several months for its completion, during the Second World War, maps were produced on the principle of the assembly line. The many kinds of detailed data necessary in military mapping were prepared simultaneously by independent

104

units, put on transparent acetate sheets, and then all photographed together.

In view of my experience with type and printing, I was given the responsibility to get army gazetteers into print with the greatest possible urgency. The data—geographical names and coordinates—was compiled at the Department of the Interior. The production problem was roughly comparable to producing twenty or thirty dictionaries in a few months at a time when men and equipment were hard to find. My typographic connections proved of value, and I was able to induce several large book manufacturing plants to commit their facilities to the gazetteers; then called on Charles Proffitt, Director of the Columbia University Press, who agreed to devote the full personnel of their encyclopedia staff for checking and proofreading. It worked. The gazetteers arrived in the field on time, including those for the entire coast of northern France.

Washington was a cultural desert during wartime. Fortunately Carl Wheat, an aficionado of fine printing, friend and patron of the Grabhorn Press in California, found about two dozen people involved in the war effort in Washington who were professionally concerned with books, and who responded with alacrity and zest to a proposed monthly dinner meeting of good food, good drink, and talk about books. He found a senator from New Mexico, Clinton P. Anderson, a book collector; army colonel John T. Winterich, writer and literary historian; Sidney Kramer, writer and bookseller; James D. Hart, historian and amateur printer who later became a Vice-Chancellor of the University of California at Berkeley; and others including a grateful typographer temporarily at the Army Map Service. The group called themselves the Washington Order of Obfuscated Bookmen—WOOFBYs for short. Some years later when Anderson was in the Kennedy Cabinet, we met briefly at the large Washington dinner for Robert Frost. He not only remembered; he said he never willingly missed a WOOFBY evening.

The war came to an end in 1945 and it was time to return to old and more familiar patterns. But the Second World War marked the beginning of enormous changes in society, both sociological and technological. The vast and awesome cloud from the atomic bomb that exploded over Hiroshima has symbolized, it seems to me, the gigantism that has spread over the world. Most of the ills—bigness, overpopulation, crime, inflation, unemployment—accelerated and have become world problems since the close of a war that claimed more than thirty million lives.

THE METROPOLITAN MUSEUM OF ART AND THE MUSEUM PRESS

Henry Watson Kent was an important participant in the cultural life of New York during the first half of the present century. He came to New York from Massachusetts in 1900, a trained librarian. After five years at the Grolier Club in that capacity, he joined the administrative staff of the Metropolitan Museum. From 1913 to 1940 he was its noted and rather formidable Secretary. Always drawn to the world of the book, Kent became an active president of the Grolier Club, 1920 to 1924, and of the American Institute of Graphic Arts, 1936 to 1938. In discharging these responsibilities, he met De Vinne, Updike, Rogers, Rollins, and other scholarly practitioners who became his typographic associates and close friends. Kent found in himself a love of elegant printing, and, surprisingly perhaps, the desire and capacity to produce it.

Dissatisfied with the bland handwritten labels that had described objects in the Museum's showcases, and the lack of character in the Museum's printed matter, Kent proceeded to buy type and presses and established the Museum Press in the Museum's basement. In his memoirs, *What I Am Pleased to Call My Education* (1949), he wrote: "We eventually got a full complement of machinery and did everything needed for the Museum except the *Bulletin* and books— posters, forms and blanks, invitations, pamphlets, and of course labels." The

106

carefully chosen types in use at the Museum Press included Bruce Rogers' Centaur, which Kent helped to bring about; Frederic Warde's Arrighi, to which Kent also lent support; the noble Bremer Presse Greek; and a font of Egyptian hieroglyphics.

The excellent work that was done at the Museum Press received the recognition it deserved in a comprehensive exhibition at the Pierpont Morgan Library in New York in 1938. Belle da Costa Greene, its astute librarian, stated that the exhibition was "in appreciation of the work initiated and furthered by Mr. Kent in raising the standard of institutional printing to that of one of the Fine Arts." At the opening of the exhibition, laudatory addresses were delivered by Mr. Kent's most distinguished colleagues. I was in the audience that special evening. How little could I then have imagined that twenty-eight years later the Morgan Library—imposing cathedral of the book—would again recognize a living American printer with, in 1966, an exhibition called "The Spiral Press Through Four Decades."

The Cloisters, magnificent outpost of the Metropolitan Museum of Art in its striking medieval building on a commanding height overlooking the Hudson River, was formally opened to a distinguished gathering on the tenth of May 1938. The speakers were George Blumenthal, President of the Museum; Fiorello H. LaGuardia, Mayor of the City of New York; Robert Moses, Commissioner of Parks; and John D. Rockefeller, Jr., the munificent donor. After paying glowing tribute to all participants, Mr. Rockefeller said, "Thanks are due not primarily to me, for my part in the undertaking, being largely financial, has been relatively unimportant." The following day Mr. Kent asked me to make a book of the addresses in an edition of 250 copies. He proposed no conditions as to design. We hand-set the speeches in Emerson foundry type and printed on dampened Etruria handmade paper. I recall an excessively humid summer because the printed sheets when hung to dry in our shop did so with great reluctance. However, during October the books were finally bound and delivered. Two years later Kent retired. Not long thereafter, without its guiding spirit, the Museum Press was dismantled, the machinery and equipment sold. Almost forty years later, by an extraordinary set of circumstances, following a neighbor's death, the original Centaur matrices and the Arrighi punches were found only a few miles from my home in West Cornwall. I identified those "strange pieces of metal" and was instrumental in having them presented to the Cary collection in the School of Printing at the Rochester Institute of Technology.

The Kent tradition of typographic comeliness was remembered and respected when the Museum turned to outside designers and printers. Until our own closing in 1971, the Museum was one of the pillars that kept a dry roof over the Spiral Press. I designed and printed some of the Museum publications, much of the ephemera, and saw their printing needs take on very large proportions as their activities kept pace with the cultural revolution. Three books printed and bound for the Museum may be recalled. *Ching Ming Shang Ho*, a Chinese scroll of a spring festival on a river, was made into a portfolio in 1948 at the request of Marshall B. Davidson, Editor of Publications. *The Belles Heures of Jean, Duke of Berry, Prince of France* (1958), including color reproductions made by Draeger Frères in Paris, was several times reprinted. *Aesop, Five Centuries of Illustrated Fables* (1964), designed by our associate Peter Oldenburg, reached total printings of some forty thousand copies. For many years, under the direction of Bradford D. Kelleher, we printed more than a million Christmas cards each year. These were chosen from the Museum collections, chiefly medieval and Renaissance woodcuts and decorations that were restored and retouched, where necessary, by Fritz Kredel, himself an eminent wood engraver. I designed and set up the advertisements for newspapers and magazines for the cards and other objects that were sold in the admirable Museum store, where extraordinarily faithful reproductions of pottery, statuettes, jewelry, and other artifacts in the Museum collections were made

108

available to people who could never even dream of possessing the priceless originals.

STEUBEN GLASS

Arthur A. Houghton, Jr., a member of the family that built the giant Corning Glass works, set out in the thirties with a newly developed formula and with a small group of skilled workmen experienced in the ancient craft of glass blowing, "to make the finest glass the world had ever seen." He called on his friends, architect John M. Gates and sculptor Sidney Waugh, to join him at Steuben Glass with the objective of bringing visionary contemporaneous form to "crystal of matchless purity and design." World War II intervened.

In 1946, after discharge from the United States Air Force, Houghton came to see me on the suggestion of Philip Hofer, collector of rare illustrated books, then at work at Harvard's Houghton Library. Houghton wanted to know what needed to be done to establish a private press at his farm in Maryland with a serious editorial and production program committed to the arts of the book. After an hour or two of discussion concerning type, presses, paper, binding, distribution, and personnel, Houghton decided that he would rather devote such energies to wider fields of service in the arts. This he did when, among other pursuits, he became President of the Metropolitan Museum of Art, a working trustee of the New York Public Library, and actively associated with many other cultural institutions.

Houghton had another, more immediate problem. He was finding it difficult to get printing done that would reflect the idealism and artistry that he and his associates were giving to the production of glass. He had tried Madison Avenue without success. Would I, he asked, take on the assignment? A few weeks later, at a meeting at Steuben Glass headquarters over their lavish shop on Fifth Avenue, a vast accumulation of material to be printed was laid out. I hesitated, but Houghton asked me to proceed with its design and production and to move the work along as quickly as might be possible. Three years were required to establish a style and to finish the many books and booklets, catalogues, brochures, corporate stationery, and other printed matter. No Steuben device (or logo as it is usually called) then existed, and I suggested that a meaningful, decorative design would provide a distinguishing motif that would tie their printed matter together. Houghton proposed a snow crystal. I asked Philip Grushkin, a free-lance designer often associated with the Spiral Press, to submit a sketch. His ingenious solution, immediately accepted, was a decided typographic asset. It also became the successful and familiar Steuben corporate trademark.

The Steuben relationship began well and remained active and exciting for about twenty years. In addition to the many fine vases, bowls, and other glass objects designed by Gates, Waugh, and other early members of the Steuben staff, many of the world's prominent artists were asked to participate. Designs from Eric Gill, Jean Cocteau, Isamu Noguchi, Leon Kroll, and others were engraved on glass. Karl Kup, Curator of the Spencer Collection at the New York Public Library, was sent to the Far and Near East to assemble contemporary work that became an exhibition, "Asian Artists in Crystal." Typical of Houghton's initiative to bring several of the arts together was a project in the early sixties called "Poetry in Crystal." Through the Poetry Society of America, Steuben invited virtually all of America's best-loved poets to submit new verse which would be illustrated or interpreted on abstract glass forms of imagination and beauty by sympathetic artists, designers, and engravers. Thirty-one poets responded. Among them were W. H. Auden, Marianne Moore, William Carlos Williams, Mark Van Doren, Conrad Aiken, and Robinson Jeffers. It was my good fortune to be involved in these creative projects, which called for printed matter and rather sumptuous illustrated, bound catalogues—the best possible grist for the Spiral Press mill.

110

As Steuben became a kind of national institution, and its glass became a touchstone for an affluent society, their printing needs went far beyond our limited resources. But before Arthur Houghton retired from its active administration, he asked me to design the proposed publication of the marvelous sixteenth-century Persian illuminated manuscript, *Shahnameh* ("Book of Kings"), which he had acquired. After fifteen years in production (with designer Peter Oldenburg carrying on), two scholarly folio volumes, magnificently illustrated, were issued in 1981 by the Harvard University Press for two thousand dollars.

My debt to "glass of matchless purity and design" was not forgotten. When my home was built in the woods of northwest Connecticut, I rejected ordinary window glass and, despite the extra expense, chose plate glass so that we might look to the distant Berkshire hills through windows the clearest and the purest.

INSTITUTIONS AND FOUNDATIONS

As already mentioned, museums, libraries, educational institutions, and foundations provided the steady work that kept our presses running from year to year as they did at other small printing houses. Because such institutions were normally directed and staffed by persons of discrimination, with concerns that were wholly or in part cultural, they would logically want well-designed printing. And because they were not watched by hungry stockholders and controlled by unduly frugal treasurers, they could enjoy good workmanship without apology.

The Twentieth Century Fund, established in 1919 by the Boston merchant Edward A. Filene for the purpose of "conducting research and public education on economic and social problems," had a board of directors composed of exceptional men prominent in public life, and several distinguished directors, including one who was an expert, if amateur, craft printer.

The Fund's many research projects conducted by economists and scholars were published by the Fund in book form. I designed most of these studies which were printed by book manufacturing plants. At the Spiral Press I redesigned the Fund's stationery, designed and printed the book jackets, posters, brochures, and other matter pertinent to a publishing program. And I arranged for a new Fund logo, which George Salter designed very successfully with superb calligraphic skill.

In 1956, when August Heckscher became the Director, a very good relationship became even better due to his own typographic gifts and enthusiasm. Every printing project became a stimulating challenge. Among his public activities, Heckscher was Consultant in the Arts for President Kennedy and a Commissioner of Parks who planted thousands of trees in New York City. In his living room in New York, he set type by hand and printed fine small books and ephemera, often with the help of his son Charles. More recently he has set up "The Printing Office at High Loft" at his summer home in Seal Harbor, Maine, where with young apprentices he prints and publishes modestly but with éclat.

America's most honored writers, artists, architects, and musicians, members of the American Academy and Institute of Arts and Letters, gather each year in May at their beautiful building in New York for their annual "Ceremonial," which according to their recent president "marks our mission to honor and nurture the arts in America." Here these native immortals salute the newly elected members, present medals for conspicuous achievement, distribute cash awards to talented aspirants, and listen to a speech by a contemporary sage on the state of the world. Then, under a large canopy on their terrace, they mix food and drink and much good talk with assembled friends and guests. May no misguided bomb ever fall on this concentration of America's most celebrated practitioners in the arts!

The Board of Directors of this venerable body once took time to pass a resolution commending the Spiral Press for a newly designed letterhead. The relationship had begun in 1940 when Van Wyck Brooks, writer and literary historian, wanted Academy-Institute printing to relate to their purposes. The Academy recognized the art of the book when in 1948 their gold medal was awarded to Bruce Rogers for his work in the graphic arts.

Our first commission was a book of more than 400 pages, *Commemorative Tributes of the American Academy of Arts and Letters, 1905–1941*. Here were printed the words from a period of only thirty-six years when living members memorialized 119 of their dead. As I specified type for the table of contents, the grim sequences became apparent—with what certainty, he who spoke would all too soon be spoken about. For thirty years we produced the catalogues for many exhibitions, the annual *Proceedings*, and much other printed matter required by an active cultural institution.

The Frick Collection in its exquisite building on Fifth Avenue overlooking Central Park, with its great paintings, its Sunday afternoon concerts, its flowered central pool, is an enchanted oasis in a city given over to bigness, noise, and haste. This small museum is a classic essence of grace and nobility. When, about 1950, the Director, Frederick Mortimer Clapp, called me to his office and asked me to take over their printing and give it some distinction, I was enormously pleased.

In the *Handbook of Paintings* of 1971 (printed at the Spiral Press) the Director, Harry D. M. Grier, wrote: "The Frick Collection was founded by Henry Clay Frick (1849–1919), the Pittsburgh coke and steel industrialist. At his death Mr. Frick bequeathed his New York residence and the finest of his works of art to establish a public gallery of art for the purpose of 'encouraging and developing the study of the Fine Arts.' Among the numerous works bequeathed by Mr. Frick were one hundred thirty-one paintings. Since that time thirty-eight additional paintings have been purchased by the Trustees from an endowment provided by Mr. Frick."

113

As with other institutions without a staff designer, I really became an adjunct member of the organization. Relations with Frick directors and staff remained very cordial and productive until the Spiral Press closed down, and even beyond when I was asked for occasional typographic advice. In 1968 I was invited to give a lecture in their series on art, "Saturdays at Three," in their elegant auditorium. The subject was "The Great Printed Book From Gutenberg to the Oxford Lectern Bible."

The New York office of the American Academy in Rome was a faithful customer for many years with annual reports, promotional literature, and all the other printed matter needed for their programs that sent promising young American artists, musicians, and architects to their beautiful buildings in Rome. The women at Vassar College gave serious thought to printing for ceremonial anniversaries. For their fiftieth year they turned to Daniel Berkeley Updike, for the seventy-fifth to Peter Beilenson, for their centennial to the Spiral Press. Our relations with Manhattanville College began when a new president wanted her inaugural program to have some distinction.

Our largest commission originated in the offices of the Bollingen Foundation in New York. It was finally completed and published twelve years later by the Yale University Library in New Haven. As a memorial to his wife, Mary Conover Mellon, Paul Mellon presented to Yale the rare collection of books on alchemy which Mrs. Mellon had acquired during her close association with C. G. Jung, the noted Swiss physician and psychologist. Jung wrote that "alchemy gains the quite new and interesting aspect of a *projected psychology of the collective unconscious*, and thus ranks with mythology and folklore. Its symbolism is in the closest relation to dream symbolism on the one hand, and to the symbolism of religion on the other." Mr. Mellon directed that a full-scale, illustrated bibliographical catalogue of the collection be prepared as part of the memorial gift and for the benefit of historical scholarship. The collection comprised

149 manuscripts written between the years 1225 and 1922, and 160 books printed from 1472 to 1790.

From the start I was a member of the committee responsible for procedures and publication. The committee was chaired by James T. Babb, Librarian of Yale University. Meetings were held at the Beinecke Library, Yale's rare books division in its own beautiful building with transluscent marble walls. My special duties were, of course, design and overall production. The esoteric nature of the subject matter necessitated a complex editorial apparatus. The final publication, entitled *Alchemy and the Occult* and subtitled "A Catalogue of Books and Manuscripts From the Collection of Paul and Mary Mellon," required four volumes with 1600 pages, 9 ⅛ x 12 ¼ inches.

Volumes one and two, which described the books, were compiled by bibliographer Ian MacPhail, who spent two full years on the assignment. Included in the final publication in 1968 was an introduction by Robert Multhauf of the Smithsonian Institution, an essay by Aniela Jaffé, who had been Jung's secretary and assistant, and references by William McGuire to Jung's collected works. The Bembo type, which I chose for its classical background, was printed at the Spiral Press. The reproductions were printed at the Meriden Gravure Company, probably the last time their collotype presses were used.

The extremely difficult compilation of the manuscript volumes (published in 1977) was accomplished by Laurence C. Witten II. The search for an editor knowledgeable in early European languages settled on my associate Joseph Bernstein, himself a Yale graduate who had specialized in medieval speech. An historical introduction came from Pearl Kibre, and Witten contributed a detailed essay on the formation of the collection and cataloguing procedures.

Inasmuch as the Spiral Press had closed while this undertaking was in work, the two final volumes were set in type at the Stinehour Press. Because of the many reproductions interspersed with type, it was decided to print type and plates simultaneously at Meriden. However, I directed our good friends at Stinehour to pull letterpress proofs, fully made ready and printed with normal impression on the final paper on which the books later would be printed by offset. The aura of adequate coverage would thus be held in the offset printing. I believe that the reason so much poor offset printing is produced is due to the inadequacy of type pulled by proof boys on coated paper, or the excessively sharp images on film of contrasting type design.

On the completion of his editorial labors, Ian MacPhail concluded his page of acknowledgments with a sentence about Paul Mellon (Yale class of 1929): "The most unobtrusive of Maecenases, he has placed us all immeasurably in his debt." I should like to add "and the most considerate." On 29 September 1978 he wrote to me: "I have been overjoyed by your care and sensitivity in carrying out the production of all four volumes. I know that Mary, too, would have been delighted with this beautiful summation of her great interest in alchemy, and would have been very proud, as I am, to have been connected with the enterprise. Many, many thanks."

THE GROLIER CLUB

"On the evening of Wednesday, January twenty-third, 1884, nine men of kindred tastes but of considerable disparity in years met in the library of a substantial brownstone residence at 11 East Thirty-sixth Street, far above the hurlyburly of downtown New York." Thus begins *The Grolier Club, 1884–1967: An Informal History* by John T. Winterich. The Club's nine founding fathers were Theodore Low De Vinne, printer; Robert Hoe, Jr., a manufacturer of printing presses who built a library of 150,000 volumes; four men who edited, printed, and published books and magazines; and three lawyer-banker-collectors, one of whom owned a Gutenberg Bible. For their patron saint and namesake they chose Jean Grolier of Lyons (1479–

1565), treasurer-general of France, friend of Aldus, patron of learning and the arts, whose books were magnificently bound by the legendary craftsmen of Italy and France. Each book was stamped in gold, *Io. Grolierii et amicorum*—Jean Grolier and his friends. The object of the Club was to be "the literary study and promotion of the arts pertaining to the production of books." If these worthy purposes were meant to include the pursuits of book collecting and preservation, the founding fathers were indeed men of foresight.

The Club now has more than 600 members spread nationwide, representing the many aspects of the book. It is now elegantly housed in its five-story building on East Sixtieth Street with excellent facilities for exhibitions and meetings. Its library contains some 70,000 volumes and 15,000 prints. Accepting its responsibilities as an educational institution and enjoying its pleasures as a social group, the Club has mounted several major exhibitions each year open to the public, as well as smaller exhibitions for its members. These exhibitions, usually very impressive, are organized by the Club's many professionals. They fall into four general categories: literary, pictorial, bibliographic, and typographic.

The Club has never failed to honor and sustain its original commitment to the printed page. Its many publications (books and exhibition catalogues) have from the first been produced with the greatest care. For example, in the spirit of typographic adventure, in 1921 the Club commissioned six of "America's most eminent printers," each to use a text of his own choosing and to make an edition without restrictions of 300 copies for the membership. The men and the books were Bruce Rogers, *The Pierrot of the Minute* by Ernest Dowson; Carl Purington Rollins, *A Lodging for the Night* by Robert Louis Stevenson; T. M. Cleland, *The Compromise of the King of the Golden Isles* by Lord Dunsany; Walter Gilliss, *The Culprit Fay and Other Poems* by Joseph Rodman Drake; Frederic W. Goudy, *Three Essays* by Augustine Birrell; and John Henry Nash, *Quattrocentisteria* by Maurice Hewlett. These books after sixty years hold up

117

very well. The little Bruce Rogers *Pierrot* is a masterpiece in small format of typographic enchantment.

Soon after the Spiral Press was established I received occasional commissions from the Grolier Club to print their invitations to meetings, bookplates, and other choice assignments. Among the books that came later, my favorite is *Grolier 75*, published in 1959, a volume to celebrate the seventy-fifth anniversary of the Club. Its 240 pages contained biographical sketches of seventy-five illustrious members of the past, each written by a living member. With a limitation of 1500 words, the result was a fascinating compilation, in pungent and often witty prose, of the great men of the book in an earlier generation. Other Spiral Press books made for the Club were the Winterich history mentioned above; *What I Am Pleased to Call My Education* (1949) by Henry W. Kent; *Italian Influence on American Literature* (1962) by C. Waller Barrett; and *Eighteenth-Century Studies in Honor of Donald F. Hyde* (1970), edited by W. H. Bond.

In 1945 I became a member, in the early sixties served on the Club's Council, and in 1967 was made an honorary member. Since the start it has been a very rewarding association, which has brought friendships of great professional and warm personal significance.

THE PIERPONT MORGAN LIBRARY

A Renaissance palazzo of flawless grandeur houses The Pierpont Morgan Library in New York with its awesome collection of illuminated manuscripts, early and later printed books, bindings, autograph letters, drawings, and prints. The incredibly high level of quality of all these holdings marks the founder, J. Pierpont Morgan, albeit a financial titan, as a collector of exceptional taste, skill, and courage. Consolidation and growth of "Mr. Morgan's library," as it was then called, was furthered by his perceptive choice in 1905 of its first librarian, Belle da Costa Greene, a young cataloguer at the Princeton University Library. Firmly and brilliantly she reigned for the next forty-three years. Meantime, in 1924 the Library was incorporated by the legislature of the State of New York as an educational institution and public reference library.

My first introduction to this hospitable repository came in 1926, when I requested admission to the library to search through the lyrics of the Elizabethan poet Nicholas Breton, which became the text for our joyous slender volume, *Phillida and Coridon*. After several unsuccessful attempts during succeeding years to see Miss Greene, she finally telephoned in 1947 and asked me to call. She informed me on arrival that she found fine printers conceited and arrogant, but that she had a project in mind that needed extraspecial care. As a memorial tribute to Mr. Morgan, she wished to have the finest possible facsimile edition of William Makepeace Thackeray's wonderful Christmas fairy tale, *The Rose and the Ring*, made from the eighty-five pages of closely written and profusely illustrated manuscript in the Morgan collection. With its many enchanting watercolored drawings, also by Thackeray, it was one of Mr. Morgan's special favorites. Gordon N. Ray, a Thackeray scholar, wrote a heartwarming introduction that we set in Fairfield type. I asked the Meriden Gravure Company to make base plates of the illustrations by their collotype process, which were then hand-colored at the Martha Berrien studio by *pochoir*, a stencil method appropriately employing watercolors. With the book finally printed and bound, Miss Greene expressed her pleasure and thereafter always had a friendly word for me — but I never learned whether she had changed her mind about fine printers.

The Library was again very fortunate in its choice of directors when, in 1948, the trustees named Frederick B. Adams, Jr., to succeed Miss Greene. I had first met Adams at the Pynson Printers' teas during the early thirties when he was an editor of *The Colophon* and I was engaged in printing several of their pieces. Our relationship was also nourished by our mutual friendships with Robert Frost. Fred was a Frost collector and intimate who, at Frost's request, accompanied him on his trip to Russia in 1962 to meet Khrushchev. From that journey came the book *To Russia With Frost*. Adams wrote the text; Tom Nason made a wood engraving for the title page entwining the Russian hammer and sickle with Frost's scythe and axe; there were photographs of Frost sitting and talking with Russia's most prominent poets; I designed and printed five hundred copies in Bulmer type for Boston's Club of Odd Volumes.

One of Adams' first duties as Director was to organize an exhibition in 1949 to honor the forty-three years of Miss Greene's tenure and, concurrently, the Library's first quarter century as a public institution. The illustrated catalogue (printed at the Spiral Press) contained an introduction by scholar-librarian Lawrence C. Wroth, also bibliographies and reproductions representing the immense wealth of acquisitions made by Miss Greene.

Adams' special interest in books and printing was a boon to all concerned. In addition to editorship of *The Colophon*, he was President of the Grolier Club, served a term on the Board of Directors of the American Institute of Graphic Arts, and was a member of the Typophiles. He spread the Morgan jobs among selected printers, but the Spiral Press enjoyed the largest slices of the pie, both miscellaneous printing and books. Comprehensive, clothbound, illustrated annual reports to the Fellows of the Pierpont Morgan Library were begun in 1950 and dutifully maintained. Edited and introduced and partly written by Adams, they recorded the year's acquisitions, each new item described with literary pride by the director and the curators. Elegant catalogues, page size 9 x 12 inches, bound in buckram, were printed for regional exhibitions from the Morgan collections: *Italian Manuscripts* (1953) and *Central European Manuscripts* (1958). Texts were by Meta Harrsen, amply illustrated in black and white, and color.

If I were asked by a harassed St. Peter outside the Pearly Gates to show only one printed book on which I should be judged, I would hope to have with me the weighty volume *Chinese Calligraphy and*

Painting in the Collection of John M. Crawford, Jr. It was the most complex book of my career with a multitude of mechanical and typographic problems in English and Chinese that had to be pulled together. It was a Morgan Library publication for the exhibition, which opened there in 1962, of the wonderful examples of early Chinese art that Mr. Crawford had acquired. The ancient calligraphy was especially stirring. Since I could not read the meaning, these free and mysterious forms were pure abstract art.

Crawford had been a discriminating collector of private press books, notably from the Kelmscott and Doves presses, and of related material. He wanted the permanent catalogue of the exhibition to satisfy his love of fine bookmaking. Our opening meeting, arranged by Fred Adams, was held three years before the exhibition date at John Crawford's home—the first of many days spent among his beautiful objects. Scholarship had already been assured by an eminent group of specialists in Oriental art who prepared the text under the general editorship of Laurence Sickman of the William Rockhill Nelson Gallery of Art, Kansas City, Missouri. The book finally became a volume of 300 pages, text set in Garamond type, display in Zapf's Sistina; with three splendid color plates by Arthur Jaffé, New York, and fifty-one superb collotype plates by the Meriden Gravure Company. For this, as with other volumes demanding the greatest skills in printing reproductions, I turned to Harold Hugo and John Peckham at Meriden, friends and colleagues in pursuit of the maximum integration between type and plates. The paper, Caledonia Parchment, was suitable for both letterpress printing and collotype reproduction. In order to retain maximum possible size, several of the scrolls were reproduced on sheets up to three feet in length, folded and bound into the books by Frank Fortney's Russell-Rutter bindery in New York. In addition to the full-scale catalogue, a small format paperbound, directed to students at a low price, was also made for gallery sale.

When—about 1960—the facilities of the Morgan Library were

again inadequate, a second expansion plan was undertaken which provided modern atmospheric controls, a handsome new lecture hall, additional space for stacks, offices for curators, and other benefits. The architect of the new building, Alexander P. Morgan, a great-nephew of the Founder, came up with the happy thought that a frieze of printers' marks would be appropriate adornment for the new small exhibition room and sales area. At this point Mrs. Sherman P. Haight proposed that the Hroswitha Club, a group of women book collectors, would provide the funds for the frieze in memory of Belle Greene, who had been one of the Club's founders. Sixteen devices would thereby be carved in wood, high on these noble walls.

In the booklet *Printers' Marks in the Pierpont Morgan Library* Adams tells how he and Curt Bühler, Curator of Early Printed Books, made the difficult selections. Some were "immediately obvious; others, notably Gutenberg and Updike, had no marks and had to be omitted; several devices were too complicated." The final choice of twelve printers from earlier centuries were Johann Fust & Peter Schoeffer, Erhard Ratdolt, Aldus Manutius, William Caxton, Richard Pynson, Schoolmaster Printer of St. Albans, Antoine Vérard, Simon Vostre, Plantin Press, Elzevier Press, Octavianus Scotus, and Juan Rosenbach. With deference to their time and place, four contemporary Americans were added: Bruce Rogers, Pynson Printers (Elmer Adler), Thistle Press, and Spiral Press. At the evening opening in 1962 of the new quarters, Adams casually led me to the frieze and slyly pointed to the north wall where the Spiral triskelion would spend eternity between the monograms of Caxton and the Elzeviers. I was flabbergasted and inordinately proud. I could hardly question the choices! Parenthetically, it gives me pleasure to note that the Spiral is one of several printers' marks that Walter Frankel, Librarian at the Taft School in Watertown, Connecticut, ordered in glass sculpture cast by Priscilla Manning Porter. They hang, illuminated by the tall sunlit windows of the beautiful new Taft library.

One day in 1965 Fred Adams startled me with the news that the Morgan Library wished to hold an exhibition the next year whose title was to be "The Spiral Press Through Four Decades." He anticipated a comprehensive retrospective exhibition of Spiral Press printing that would remain on view in their main gallery for about two months. I refused to believe that the work I had done during the preceding forty years could be shown within walls that housed the world's most magnificent illuminated manuscripts and noblest printed books. But Adams insisted, and we chose sixty of my best printed books, also miscellaneous job work (ephemera) of all kinds from business cards to catalogues and annual reports that filled the cases and the walls. In order to enliven the show, we included work in progress, original drawings, engraving tools, punches and smoke proofs of Emerson type, and thanks to the Library at Hyde Park the typescripts for the five introductions to the Roosevelt State Papers with the President's handwritten corrections.

I was asked to write the exhibition labels. It was expected, with mercy to the anticipated reviewing audience, that the data would present lively information in commendable brevity concerning type and paper and its relation to contemporary American printing. As I dug back to my beginnings, sentences fell into chronological sequence and, pieced together, became a sort of autobiography of a printing house. Adams urged that they could logically be the source for an introductory essay for the catalogue. Whereupon—lo and behold—a book came into being. The catalogue finally contained one hundred pages, with forty-four pages devoted to "Notes on the Spiral Press," the balance for bibliographies, reproductions of pieces printed at the Spiral Press, and a showing of Emerson type. The edition consisted of 400 copies hardbound in cloth and 1500 copies paperbound. The cloth sold out before the exhibition closed, the paperbound soon thereafter. The London *Times Literary Supplement* of 16 June 1966 reviewed *The Spiral Press Through Four Decades* with a knowledgeable glance at American printing and added: "This is in fact an agreeably phrased chronicle not only of the activities of the Spiral Press, but of the stylistic and technical development of the young man who started as a salesman for B. W. Huebsch in 1924 and is today in grave danger of becoming, prematurely, the doyen of eastern seaboard printers."

The exhibition opened on a snowy evening, the twenty-sixth of January 1966. Nevertheless, 270 people came, in black tie and elegant long skirts. In a review of the event, the *Journal of the American Institute of Graphic Arts* reported that the opening "was attended by collectors and booksellers, and by compositors, pressmen and other craftsmen of the graphic arts, all of whom were present to honor one of their own." August Heckscher was the generous speaker of the evening. His talk began, "It is a privilege to open this exhibition. Yet the speaker on such a night must feel superfluous. Like all good work, the work of the Spiral Press speaks for itself, if we but look at it attentively and let it tell its own story. However, the occasion imposes some obligation upon me, and I shall during the brief moments to come speak a little of Mr. Blumenthal, a little of the things he has made, and before I am through say something of the meaning of all this for the age we live in." It was a good evening for the aficionados and practitioners who came and saw the Morgan Library honor their cherished craft; it was a magical evening for me.

After twenty-one years in charge, Adams resigned and the trustees found their third brilliant Director, Charles Ryskamp, Professor of English at Princeton University with bibliographic and bibliophilic leanings. Before the administrative changeover, a fine exhibition, "Bookbindings of T. J. Cobden-Sanderson," was held in 1969. Almost all of the reproductions in Morgan catalogues had been done for us by the Meriden Gravure Company by collotype or in duotone 300-line-screen offset. But for the Cobden-Sanderson bindings I wanted, as far as possible, to hold the luster of gold and the sheen of leather. This we achieved by letterpress at the Spiral Press with halftone plates on high-coated paper. The *Times* of London com-

124

mented (11 June 1970): "The catalogue itself is a handsome production well up to the high standards we have come to expect from the Spiral Press, and the thirty-six plates are of especially excellent quality." There were 1350 copies, paperbound.

The last catalogue of the Adams tenure was prepared secretly by the curatorial staff and printed by us without the Director's knowledge. *A Review of Acquisitions, 1949–1968* was made to celebrate the extraordinary growth of the Morgan Library during the Adams years. Fred was utterly surprised and overwhelmed when (in 1969) the completed volume was presented to him. Printed in Baskerville and Bulmer types, 1000 copies were clothbound, 2000 copies paperbound. I find that during the last decade of my career I turned principally to Baskerville and Bulmer. Both faces, eminently readable, were designed in England during the eighteenth century. I found them fresh, crisp and cultivated in design, not directly related to traditional Renaissance pen forms like the excellent Bembo nor the sophisticated finality of Bodoni. Both English types are stylistically related, with Bulmer's slightly stronger weight giving subtle and welcome emphasis.

Charles Ryskamp's partiality to the well-printed book was already in evidence during his close association with the Princeton University Press and its top-notch designer, P. J. Conkwright. Soon after taking hold at the Morgan Library, he would write in one of the catalogues: "At a time when libraries and museums seem less concerned about the typography of their publications, we have tried to maintain and, if possible, to improve the quality of our printing and our photographic reproductions." Whereupon the shades of Gutenberg and Aldus who haunted the Library stacks during interregnums were reassured and returned to rest within the covers of their books.

Two substantial Morgan exhibition catalogues were completed before the Spiral Press closed its doors. The *Mary Flagler Cary Music Collection* (1970) provided one of the thrills of a lifetime. In the course

125

of production I handled the very sheets on which Beethoven, Bach, Mozart, Chopin, and others had written their imperishable music. *Artists and Writers* (1971) was a showing of portrait drawings from the collection of Benjamin Sonnenberg. Two catalogues followed which I handled as a free-lance designer: *The Blake Collection of Mrs. Landon K. Thorne* (1971) and *English Drawings and Watercolors, 1550– 1850* (1972) in the collection of Mr. and Mrs. Paul Mellon.

LIQUIDATION AND DISPERSAL

A combination of circumstances, some rather personal, provided clear signals that after forty-five typographic years the time had come to stop the presses. Hence, in 1971 the Spiral Press was liqui- dated. People and machines long together soon went their separate ways.

When I called used-machinery dealers with the expectation that they might buy our presses, I was quickly informed that letterpress equipment was obsolete and totally unsalable. What did they ad- vise? "Call a junkie. They will cut up your presses with acetylene torches and a sledgehammer and cart them away—at a price." I shuddered, but the typographic gods above came to our rescue. The Stinehour Press in Vermont wanted our cylinder press and the Kluge automatic; David Godine took our Miehle Horizontal and the paper cutter to his barn in Brookline, Massachusetts; and I pre- sented our 14 x 22 Colts Armory press to the Pierson Press at Yale, where a fine group of undergraduates still pursues the art and mys- tery of printing with scholarly determination and high spirits during extracurricular hours. In appreciation of the gift, I was made a Fellow of Pierson College for five years. The perquisites allowed dining in their cafeteria and a dormitory bed if available. Indeed, one evening after the printers' spring wayzgoose, my wife and I enjoyed the comfortable guest suite in the master's house.

Much of our foundry type was picked out by several youngsters with presses in their basements. The best of it was purchased by Ed Lathem of Dartmouth College who had type, cabinets, and appurtenances trucked to his home in Hanover, from which he will one day cajole literary and typographic surprises. His lode included the initial letters I had designed and a complement of the swelled, or Bodoni, dashes cut in brass, which had become a kind of signature for Spiral Press typography. Finally, tons of leads and slugs and old standing jobs seemed to pour out of the walls—all sold for scrap metal.

The Press of A. Colish (where a generation back Abe Colish was a skillful printer for Bruce Rogers and T. M. Cleland) engaged three of my associates faithful to the end—Frank Petrocelli, Jim O'Hagan, and Harry Bettum. John Luciani, Norman Richardson, and Rae Smith had other plans. Margo Biow moved from our office to an executive post at the Metropolitan Museum of Art to become involved in the production of Museum publications. As for me, I felt like the farmer who is relieved of milking his cows seven days of every week. Suddenly I had time at my disposal, and an old dream could be realized. In the years ahead I would spend uncounted hours with the work of the great printers of history and turn the pages of their imperishable books.

ART OF THE PRINTED BOOK

In 1924 the Metropolitan Museum of Art staged a very large exhibition in New York called "Arts of the Book," organized by its highly articulate Curator of Prints, W. M. Ivins. The exhibition ran a wide gamut from spectacular Medieval and Renaissance illuminated manuscripts, through five centuries of typographic and illustrated books, to jewelled and other masterpieces of binding. Almost fifty years later it seemed to me that it was most desirable, if not actually imperative, to mount another exhibition that would show practitioners and the public the glory of the great printed books done by and since Gutenberg. I suggested to Fred Adams that the Morgan Library, with all its printed treasures, should fill the void. He warmed to the thought, and we gathered together a committee of respected colleagues to sit down with us and talk. Those who came were Alvin Eisenman of Yale; Ray Nash, Dartmouth; Alan Fern, the Library of Congress; James Wells, the Newberry Library, Chicago; and Herman Cohen, the Chiswick Bookshop, New York.

Suggestions of work to be shown ranged from papyrus rolls to contemporary paperbacks. Nothing concise and homogeneous came together, as is perhaps the fate of committee compromise. Whereupon Adams said, "Why don't you do it yourself." But I was still running a printing shop. When I was ready to accept, Fred had resigned and moved to Europe.

Early in his directorship, Charles Ryskamp responded to my proposal with enthusiasm. Granted that the selection of books would be mine, Ryskamp's staunch support was sustained all the way to the ceremonial opening. The exhibition, to be called "Art of the Printed Book," would be limited to significant and distinguished work produced during the five hundred years since the invention of movable type—Gutenberg's legacy to mankind in the long search for the means of preserving and disseminating human knowledge.

Neither a librarian nor an historian nor an academic scholar, I sat down at a corner desk in the Morgan Library in the late spring of 1971 and faced the responsibilities I had taken on. The first task was self-education. My primary assets were respect for the book and some knowledge of printing. In order to understand the cultural and other forces that produced the need for the invention of printing, and to obtain some familiarity with the problems faced by the early printers, it was mandatory to read at considerable length in the history of Medieval and Renaissance Europe. There was need, too, to supplement the cursory knowledge one accumulates along the way with systematic study of the seminal printers and designers. To that end, the literature of the history of printing and its esthetics was abundant and rewarding. Furthermore, descriptive catalogues and checklists were available of such exhibitions as the Ivins selections just mentioned; a Huntington Library exhibition, "Great Books in Great Editions," San Marino, 1954; and that extraordinary showing at the British Museum in London in 1963, "Printing and the Mind of Man," with 194 examples from 1455 to 1962, from Gutenberg to Mardersteig.

In order to be able to make the final selections for the exhibition, my goal was nothing less than to see and handle every volume reputed to be among the most beautiful and typographically most important ever printed. The search was a great personal experience and enormously gratifying. Almost every book of typographic fame from the fifteenth century to the nineteenth was to be found, always in excellent condition, in the amazing Morgan stacks. The extraordinary resources of the New York Public Library and the extensive collections at Yale's elegant Beinecke Library filled in the few open spots. In the end, one sixteenth-century book was borrowed from each institution for the exhibition, and a few twentieth-century volumes came from New York collectors.

Kenneth Nesheim, the Associate Director of the Beinecke Rare Book and Manuscript Library, was most helpful in satisfying my wish as a printer to have some insight into the daily output of the printing shops in Paris and Lyons during the first half of the sixteenth century—that golden age in the history of printing. The Beinecke staff found a considerable number of small books from the Estienne, Colines, Vascosan, Tory, and de Tournes workshops. These books in small format are the direct ancestors of our modern trade books. Nevertheless, the great quartos and folios would be the most prominent showpieces in the exhibition.

Finally chosen were one hundred and eleven books (not all large format) from eighty-five printers and designers. They filled the cases of the Morgan Library's main gallery, the entrance lobby, and the vaulted East Room in 1973 from the eleventh day of September to

129

the second of December. The Gutenberg Bible in its two majestic vellum volumes was the central pinnacle that finally greeted more than thirty thousand visitors. Four books printed by Aldus Manutius were needed to show his new greek, roman and italic types (designed by Francesco Griffo) and his beautiful, illustrated *Hypnerotomachia Poliphili*. There were three books by Robert Estienne, greatest of scholar-printers, and three each to show the varied work of Jean de Tournes, Giambattista Bodoni, Pierre Didot, Francis Meynell, and Bruce Rogers. Two books each came from Fust and Schoeffer, Nicolaus Jenson, Anton Koberger, Geoffroy Tory, Simon de Colines, Christopher Plantin, the Imprimerie Royale, John Baskerville, William Bulmer, William Pickering, and William Morris. That left one book each from sixty-six designers and printers which, all together, represented the peaks of craftsmanship and artistic accomplishment during five hundred years.

In making the selections, no consideration was given to literary content. But a quick glance at the list of titles would show that Homer, the Bible, Virgil, Chaucer, Shakespeare, and their kind dominated the exhibition. Clearly, only a great text will evoke great bookmaking. Conversely, it would be idle, if not impossible, to attempt a noble typographic effort from an ignoble text. The text — the shape and meaning of the words — is the substance to which the typographic designer gives form. That, I believe, is the heart of the matter.

Preparation of a catalogue grew into a book. There was then no volume in print for students at an affordable price with a concise text and adequate illustrations. And nothing existed in print that showed the extraordinary holdings of printed books at the Morgan Library. Ryskamp encouraged me to prepare a publication that would serve both needs. With the opening of the exhibition we were able to offer a substantial paperbound volume, *Art of the Printed Book*, *1455–1955*, on a generous 9 x 12 ¼ inch page, with an historical text of some 27,000 words and 125 full-page plates. I designed the book in Monotype Baskerville with Bulmer for headings and Perpetua for display. The text was printed letterpress at Stinehour, with plates by Meriden. The first edition of two thousand copies at eleven-and-a-half dollars per copy was exhausted before the exhibition closed. Meantime, David R. Godine became a co-publisher for the trade with copies in cloth at twenty dollars. At this writing, three printings totaling fifteen thousand copies have been bought, with a fourth printing on press. Alas, the prices are no longer so low.

A full-page review of the exhibition appeared in the *New York Times* on 10 September 1973, headed "Books as an Art Form on View at the Morgan." The *Times* reporter, Israel Shenker, had come to West Cornwall to see me and talk about fine printing. His piece, with reproductions of several of the exhibition's title pages and typefaces (also the author's face), was sympathetic and enthusiastic. Next morning people were outside the Morgan waiting for the doors to open. The London *Times Literary Supplement* of 9 November 1973 also reviewed both the exhibition and the book. The lengthy and favorable review closed with "At the outset of his essay, Mr. Blumenthal explains that 'the art of the book unites two of man's most cherished goals. The preservation of knowledge is linked with presentation of the noblest poetry and prose in form consistent with the significance of the words.' By his exhibition at the Pierpont Morgan Library, and also by means of its commemorative publication, Mr. Blumenthal has convincingly demonstrated how handsomely the preservation of knowledge and the presentation of thought has been served by the art of the printed book."

THE PRINTED BOOK IN AMERICA

The high level of typographic achievement that flourished at the turn of the century in the United States had never been adequately recorded. Nor had there been a history devoted primarily to the esthetics of the craft in this country. The exhibition "Art of the

Printed Book" at the Morgan Library concerned the five hundred years of printing in the Western world. I hoped somehow to find a way to write a history of the printed book in the United States and show the volumes worthy of exhibition. Such a history would include colonial beginnings and an understanding of the background that led to the confluence of typographic genius that appeared in New England in the 1890's. It would be the story of fine printing in America, its books and its practitioners. It would not include the technology and the business of printing.

At a fortunate luncheon meeting in New York late in 1973, Edward Connery Lathem, Dean of Libraries at Dartmouth College, asked me whether I had any future projects in mind. Before we had finished a third cup of coffee, he proposed that the Dartmouth College Library would sponsor the exhibition I had just described and the book I had outlined. On his return to Hanover, I was appointed a Bibliographical Associate of the Dartmouth College Library, with my name on printed stationery and an office in which to work. Until 1977, when the exhibition "The Printed Book in America" opened and the book was published, I commuted between my home in West Cornwall and Hanover, and thoroughly enjoyed the academic association.

Any study of American printing (to which I had become committed) would start with four books: *The History of Printing in America, With a Biography of Printers and an Account of Newspapers* (1810) by Isaiah Thomas; *The Colonial Printer* (1931) by Lawrence C. Wroth; *Printing in the Americas* (1937) by John Clyde Oswald; and *The Book in America: A History of the Making and Selling of Books in the United States (1951)*, by Hellmut Lehmann-Haupt in collaboration with Lawrence C. Wroth and Rollo Silver. Each of these books is, or has recently been, available from reprint publishers. An excellent essay on American typography by James M. Wells was included in *Book Typography, 1815–1965, in Europe and the United States of America*, edited by Kenneth Day and first issued by a Netherlands printer in 1965 and published in the United States the following year by the University of Chicago Press.

The first book printed in a British-American colony was produced in a tiny, candle-lit shop on a wooden hand press that had been brought across the Atlantic by a nonconformist English minister, the Reverend Jose Glover, and set up in 1638 on the grounds of the newly established Harvard College in Cambridge, Massachusetts. *The Whole Booke of Psalmes*, known as the Bay Psalm Book, was there completed in 1640. Stephen Daye and his son Matthew, both of whom had come with Glover, composed the type for 296 pages and printed 1700 copies. Despite its errors in composition and poor presswork, the edition of the Bay Psalm Book was an astounding achievement considering the hazards of the infant colony less than twenty years after the landing in the wilderness. Only eleven copies have survived, all now reverently preserved in public institutions.

The most extraordinary work of the Cambridge Press and, indeed, of the whole colonial period was the Eliot Indian Bible. John Eliot, an English pastor settled in Roxbury, Massachusetts, felt it his mission to convert the Indians to Christianity. He preached to them in their own language, and in order to provide them with scripture, translated the entire King James Bible into the Algonquian speech expressed in roman type. With the help of a new press and type, and a new young printer, Marmaduke Johnson, sent by the English Society for Propagating the Gospel Among the Indians, printing of the entire Indian Bible, almost 1200 pages, was completed in 1663 in an incredible edition of 1500 copies. Its complete title is *Mamusse Wunneetupanatamwe Up-Biblum God, Naneeswe Nukkone Testament, Kah Wonk Wusku Testament.*

The Lenox Collection, one of the original components of the New York Public Library, contains an especially fine collection of early American printing. (Its holdings include very impressive printed work sponsored by the Church in Mexico a full hundred years before the comparatively crude printing produced in Massachusetts.)

133

From the small shops in a pioneer society, when life was restricted and survival the first consideration, from worn type and overworked presses, came the almanacs, newspapers, legal documents, and the laws of the colonial assemblies. Until the years just preceding the American Revolution, printers were wholly dependent for their presses, type, and paper on the long line of importation from England. Nevertheless, when searching through the work of our native typographic ancestors, one quickly spots the hand of the rare individual who made a conscious effort at design. Benjamin Franklin printed and published his famous book, Cicero's *Cato Major*, in 1744 with a two-color Caslon title page and, among my own favorites, his *Collection of Charters and Other Public Acts Relating to the Province of Pennsylvania* (1740). The other colonial printers whose work I found rewarding were William Parks, Virginia; James Parker, New York; John Green and J. Russell, Boston; Jonas Green, Maryland; and William Goddard, Rhode Island. The first attempt to achieve a deluxe volume was *The Columbiad* by Joel Barlow, printed in 1807 by Fry & Kammerer in Philadelphia, a quarto volume in 18-point type patterned on the Bulmer books printed in England.

The first major American printer was Isaiah Thomas (1749–1831). (Benjamin Franklin, although proud of his trade, gave up printing in his forties to serve the larger needs of his country and the world.) Isaiah Thomas, who rose from dire poverty, became an able master printer, bookbinder, paper manufacturer, bookseller, and prosperous publisher. He was, too, a colonial patriot, historian of his trade, and a public benefactor who, among other activities, founded and endowed the still-thriving American Antiquarian Society.

The nineteenth century witnessed enormous changes. A pioneer population had become a nation; machinery would take the place of age-old laborious methods; the arts and crafts would be welcomed in a society no longer preoccupied with the stark years of survival. Although there were some laudable typographic efforts during the

134

middle years of the century, I found nothing that could be considered of top rank. Technologically the picture was very different. American inventions of automatic presses and mechanical typesetting—Linotype and Monotype—affected the worldwide course of printing. But the esthetics of the craft proceeded along their own, if not wholly independent, ways.

The first significant design and workmanship on a cultural level appeared in the substantial printing plants in New York and Boston of Theodore Low De Vinne and Henry O. Houghton—both successful men of business and of scholarly attainments who smoothed the way for an heroic generation in the wings and about to take center stage. The Riverside Press in Cambridge, owned by the eminent American publishers Houghton, Mifflin & Company, drew the young Updike and then Bruce Rogers into professional book design during the 1890's. Most American book designers fell under the spell of the newly arrived Kelmscott volumes; the comely, small Mosher books were welcomed by readers of taste; Elbert Hubbard printed inspirational literature in limp-leather covers to "countless thousands"; and the young men at Harvard formed clubs for the solemn discussion of books and their proper presentation. In the ensuing years the inspired and innovative bookmaking by a young man from Indiana and the historical researches by the scion of a noted Rhode Island family would, for the first time, make important American contributions to the art of the printed book. The talented designers and printers who, together with Updike, Rogers, and Goudy, gathered in New England during the last decade of the century raised their craft to its highest significance. The succeeding fifty-year period was, surely, a heyday to celebrate, but it was only a part of the whole story that needed showing and telling.

With due ceremony, concerned people, and appropriate refreshment, the exhibition opened in May 1977 in the spacious main hall of Dartmouth's Baker Library. The final selection consisted of seventy books from sixty-four American designers and printers. The

135

exhibition fell into four chronological groups: The Colonial Period, The Nineteenth Century, The Renaissance in American Printing, and The Twentieth Century. The Bay Psalm Book and some of the other rare and fragile colonial works were represented by facsimiles, but all later volumes came from the excellent collections already in the Dartmouth Library, or acquired by Lathem for the exhibition. After two months at Hanover, the books were shown at a gala opening in October at the Bancroft Library of the University of California in Berkeley, then moved to the University of Texas, the Cornell University Library, the New York Public Library, where they were elegantly displayed in the main lobby; and the tour ended in June of 1978 at the Boston Public Library, where Roderick Stinehour spoke on "The Scholar-Printer in America." I first saw "Rocky" Stinehour in 1948 when we exchanged a few words while waiting in line for the dinner honoring Carl Rollins' retirement from his duties at Yale. Later that evening I told my wife that I had met a young man who would go far in the world of printing. This time my foresight was as good as my hindsight.

At the opening in Hanover, I was presented with the first bound copy of *The Printed Book in America*. It is a volume of 250 pages, 7¼ x 10¾ inches, with 63,000 words of text, seventy full-page plates of the seventy books in the exhibition, a bibliography, and an index. Five thousand copies were printed. David R. Godine of Boston became the publisher in association with the Dartmouth College Library. Reviews were everywhere favorable. Thomas Lask in the *New York Times*, 23 December 1977, wrote: "*The Printed Book in America* is a treasure to have and to hold." A long article prepared for the London *Times Literary Supplement* failed to appear because of their desperately long newspaper strike. A few reviewers commented that the best passages were those on the men of the "heroic generation" and the contemporary printers. This was logical; the 1890's witnessed the dawn of fine printing in America. Furthermore, I knew almost all of the great men who lived into the 1940's and be-

136

yond, and most of my contemporaries were personal friends whose printing I saw as it came along.

THE HEROIC GENERATION

The group of men who were born in the nineteenth century and whose careers began in its last decade, whose work and influence produced a great period in American printing, are the men often referred to in these pages as the heroic generation. Perhaps a few brief words about some of these cultivated and versatile artists, designers, and printers will be appropriate here. There were many other worthy practitioners. The following are the most significant.

Daniel Berkeley Updike (1860–1941), descendant of a distinguished Rhode Island family, established the Merrymount Press in Boston in 1893. During a long life he turned out books and ephemera at the highest scholarly level and gave to the printing house an eminence it had never had in the United States and rarely had elsewhere. Of the greatest importance were his contributions to the literature of his craft. Chief of these is his two-volume illustrated work, *Printing Types: Their History, Forms, and Use*, first issued by the Harvard University Press in 1922.

Bruce Rogers (1870–1957) is one of the immortals of the printed book. Born in Indiana, he joined the Riverside Press, Cambridge, Massachusetts, in 1896. There, from 1900 to 1912 he made typographic history with sixty limited editions, each a new adventure in book design that broke with the private press tradition. He designed the superb Centaur type. His later career included eight years at the Rudge printing house in Mount Vernon, New York, and close association with the Cambridge and Oxford university presses in England, where he produced several of his masterpieces, including the Oxford Lectern Bible.

Frederic W. Goudy (1865–1947), born in Bloomington, Illinois, began his career in Chicago as a lettering artist and proprietor of a small printing shop devoted to the craft. He moved to Massachusetts at the turn of the century, then to New York. He achieved fame and personal popularity with his extraordinarily prolific and successful type designs. He founded the magazine *Ars Typographica* and wrote several excellent books on the alphabet and elements of lettering, all with a deep infectious love of type and printing.

Will Bradley (1868–1962) learned the printing trade as a boy in a small Michigan mining town. At seventeen he went to Chicago and soon became a successful commercial artist. His posters made him famous. In 1895 he established and for some years conducted the Wayside Press, a printing house in Springfield, Massachusetts, where he also designed and published his own books and a magazine. Ultimately he devoted himself to magazine illustration and became art editor for the national Hearst publications.

Carl Purington Rollins (1880–1960) was New England born and bred. After some years as proprietor of the small Montague Press, Rollins accepted a call from Yale in 1918, and a year later became "Printer to Yale University" with the rank of professor. For the next thirty years he designed and supervised the production of all university printed matter as well as the books of the Yale University Press, to all of which he gave lively and scholarly distinction. He also taught at Yale and wrote with wit and charm about books and printing.

Thomas Maitland Cleland (1880–1964), a cultivated and articulate artist who served a young apprenticeship in a trade printing shop in New York, was tempted by music and the stage but finally returned to printing and the drawing board. He was an exquisite craftsman in the romantic manner of eighteenth-century France. After some years of work of "irreproachable elegance" for commerce, he devoted himself to the design and illustration of books, notably for the Limited Editions Club and the Overbrook Press.

William Addison Dwiggins (1880–1956) was a painter, woodcarver, puppeteer, calligrapher, type designer, and book designer.

138

Born in Ohio, after a few years in Chicago he settled in Hingham, Massachusetts. He gave up a very successful twenty years in advertising, then devoted his many gifts to the arts of lettering, book design, decoration and illustration, which involved an especially fruitful relationship with publisher Alfred A. Knopf. Among the several types he designed for the Mergenthaler Linotype Company, his Caledonia and Electra were the most successful.

Rudolph Ruzicka (1883–1978), born in Bohemia, grew up in Chicago, then came East. Humanist, artist, printmaker, engraver, his elegant lettering and calligraphy was seen in promotional printing, but chiefly in bookplates, posters, etc., and for book embellishment. He had a very close working relationship with Updike; he illustrated books for, among others, the Grolier and Carteret book clubs and the Lakeside Press. He designed the Fairfield and Primer types when C. H. Griffith at the Mergenthaler Linotype Company fostered American type design.

William Edwin Rudge (1876–1931) has already been discussed on page 12. His printing house, with Bruce Rogers and Frederic Warde as designers, produced much of America's finest bookmaking. The role of the Rudge plant as an invaluable seedbed has already been gratefully acknowledged.

John Henry Nash (1871–1947) carried the torch for fine printing in California during the first two decades of the present century. Born in Canada, he trained there as a compositor, and then became a professional bicycle rider. He arrived in San Francisco in 1895. After some unsuccessful partnerships he set up his own shop in 1916 and became spectacularly successful, doing large, opulent printing for West Coast millionaires and book clubs. His lavish pages were modelled on medieval illuminated manuscripts and on the great printed folios of the Renaissance.

Dard Hunter (1883–1966) came from an Ohio family of newspaper owners and printers. After nine years with Elbert Hubbard, Hunter studied and mastered handmade papermaking in England.

139

He visited surviving hand papermakers in Asia, and as a historian of primitive papermaking, wrote and compiled a number of invaluable scholarly volumes. For these books which he published, he designed and cast his own type, then also printed them on paper he had made himself, all on a high level of professional competence. His lively autobiography, *My Life With Paper* (1958), is excellent reading.

EXHIBITIONS

The Jones Library in Amherst, Massachusetts, a town library (not a part of Amherst College) with its informal and cheerful atmosphere that encouraged the children and adults of the community to read, was presided over by Charles R. Green, who very early recognized the importance of Robert Frost and collected his poetry and memorabilia. In a sunny exhibition room on the second floor, Green displayed book-related contemporary material. A small first exhibition of Spiral Press books was held there late in the thirties, then traveled to a number of libraries including the Newberry in Chicago and the Boston Public Library.

Almost twenty-five years later, George Healy, Curator of Rare Books at Cornell, and one of the many English professors who became involved in their university libraries, invited me (Cornell was my alma mater) to prepare a substantial retrospective showing of the books and ephemera I had done at the Spiral Press. In November of 1961 "Thirty-five Years of the Spiral Press" was set up in their handsome rare book rooms in the then new Olin Library building. I was proud to be asked to speak at the opening, on the beautiful campus where I had, most regrettably, been a poor student. A permanent collection of Spiral Press printed books was subsequently installed for which I was asked to provide a special bookplate.

The Morgan Library exhibition ("The Spiral Press Through Four Decades"), held in 1966, sparked a round of exhibitions abroad. The Royal Library of Belgium in Brussels and the Museum

Meermanno-Westreenianum at The Hague had jointly showed the books of Giovanni Mardersteig in 1965 and the work of Stanley Morison in 1966. H. Liebaers and C. Reedijk, directors of their respective and highly respected institutions, requested that the work shown at the Morgan Library be sent to them with a new catalogue that would include an essay by me, addressed to a European audience, on printing in the United States. The exhibitions were held in 1968. The material then went to the National Library in Edinburgh in 1970. The work came to rest in Jerusalem at the Hebrew University Library, where the curators printed a catalogue in Hebrew and English for the exhibition in 1971. At their request I presented the books and ephemera to the University for their permanent collection. I wonder if my Hebraic forefathers stirred just a bit in their desert graves.

Some years earlier, in 1957, I was able to bring together a superb collection of contemporary American printing as a gift to Sweden's typographic designers. Every spring the government-supported Graphic Institute in Stockholm — Bror Zachrisson, Director — held a week-long seminar for twenty-five especially chosen graduate designers from the four Scandinavian countries. By invitation it was conducted by a different designer-printer each year from Europe or America. I was picked for 1957. In order to bring something of real value to the Scandinavian students, I wrote to all the American designers whose work I thought warranted exhibition, and asked them to present some of their most representative work for study by their young and aspiring European colleagues. The response was extraordinarily generous, and we packed a fine assortment of American printing for shipment to Stockholm, including a small catalogue that I printed with biographical notes on the contributors. It was called *43 American Typographic Designers*. In a brief foreword I wrote: "Whether the work has been done for a museum or university press, or for the larger uses of corporate giants, there is evident here a real devotion, within an industrial society, to high standards of craftsmanship. And it is worthy of note that all these designers live from as well as by their work, for none is the product of inherited patronage or financial subsidy." It was all a great success, much appreciated by the Director of the Graphic Institute, who acknowledged the gift, and by the Royal Library, where the work was handsomely shown.

The forty-three designers and printers whose work I considered the best in the United States in 1957 should be remembered. They were John Anderson, Frederick W. Anthoensen, Leonard Baskin, Saul Bass, Herbert Bayer, Lester Beall, Bruce Beck, Peter Beilenson, Joseph Blumenthal, Will Burtin, Warren Chappell, Bert Clarke, Carroll Coleman, P. J. Conkwright, Grant Dahlstrom, Harry A. Duncan, W. A. Dwiggins, Ralph E. Eckerstrom, Alvin Eisenman, George Giusti, William Golden, Edwin and Robert Grabhorn, Victor Hammer, Walter L. Howe, Allen F. Hurlburt, Frank T. Kacmarcik, Marshall Lee, Leo Lionni, Joseph Low, Herb Lubalin, Alvin Lustig, Saul Marks, Noel Martin, Erik Nitsche, Peter Oldenburg, Paul Rand, Philip Reed, Ward Ritchie, Carl Purington Rollins, George Salter, William Stone, Ladislav Sutnar, Bradbury Thompson.

DURING the middle years of the present century, when the rising tide of the computer became a flood, we firmly believed that the ancient uses of metal type would soon become nostalgic history. We were wrong. The printing industry surrendered to film composition and offset printing, but the human spirit will never give up the delights and profound satisfactions of personal craftsmanship. A new generation has clung to the craft. Throughout the country the arts of the book have found devoted partisans who set type by hand, who make paper in handmoulds, who pull lever presses or work on hand-operated Vandercooks, and who sew and bind the printed sheets. A few intrepid practitioners continue to produce fine work on surviving letterpress equipment, and we can depend on a new breed of designers to find comfort in the computer. Despite the omnipresent airwaves that dispense entertainment and information, the alphabet and the book remain the prime sources for the preservation of knowledge and human aspiration. And so, it seems, it will continue to be.

INDEX

Abbatoir Editions, 77
Adams, Frederick B., Jr., 44, 45, 119–120, 121, 122, 123, 124, 128
Adams, Leonie, 67
Adler, Elmer, 21, 28, 43–45, 67, 88, 93, 122
Adolph Lewisohn Collection of Modern French Paintings and Sculpture, The, 20
Aesop, Five Centuries of Illustrated Fables, 108
Aesop, Twelve Fables of (Wescott), 83, 97
Aiken, Conrad, 110
Alchemy and the Occult: A Catalogue of Books and Manuscripts From the Collection of Paul and Mary Mellon, 115
Alcuin, 48
Aldine Press, 50
Aldus Manutius, 30, 49, 117, 122, 125, 130
Allen, Dorothy and Lewis, 60, 65, 93
Allen, Greer, 79
Alliger, Lewis A., 28
Alphabet of Creation, The (Samuel, trans.), 92, 96
Alphabet and Image, 46
American Academy and Institute of Arts and Letters, 25, 112–113
American Academy in Rome, 25, 115
American Antiquarian Society, 134
American Institute of Graphic Arts (AIGA), 20, 25, 31–33, 75, 79, 95, 106, 120
American Type Founders Company, 16, 26, 50, 51, 76, 100
Amsterdam Type Foundry, 37, 70
Anderson, Clinton P., 105
Anderson, Gregg, 75
Anderson, John, 142
Anderson, Sherwood, 9
Angelo, Valenti, 67, 93
Anthoensen, Frederick W., 142
Arrighi type, 52, 107, 108
Ars Typographica, 45, 138
Art of the Printed Book, 1455–1955, 130–131

Art Students League, 76, 100
Artists and Writers, 126
Arts et Métiers Graphiques, 46
Ashendene Press, 10, 50
Auden, W. H., 37, 81, 110

Babb, James T., 115
Bancroft Library, 136
Barlow, Joel, 134
Barnacles From Many Bottoms, 87
Barr, Alfred H., 83
Barrett, C. Waller, 118
Baskerville, John, 30, 88, 130
Baskerville type, 49, 50, 51, 52, 53, 63, 84, 91, 125, 131
Baskin, Leonard, 42, 83, 93, 100–101, 142
Bass, Saul, 142
Bauer Type Foundry, 34, 53, 56, 59
Bay Psalm Book, 133, 136
Bayer, Herbert, 142
Beach, Sylvia, 10
Beall, Lester, 142
Beck, Bruce, 142
Beilenson, Edna, 28
Beilenson, Peter, 28, 45, 89, 114, 142
Beinecke Rare Book and Manuscript Library, 115, 129
Bell type, 52
Belles Heures of Jean, Duke of Berry, Prince of France, The, 108
Bembo, Pietro, 49
Bembo type, 49, 52, 70, 115, 125
Bennett, Paul A., 51, 86–87, 99
Benson, John Howard, 88
Bernhard, Lucien, 34, 44, 93, 94
Bernstein, Joseph, 24, 115
Berrien, Martha, 119
Bestiary/Bestiario (Neruda), 97
Bettum, Harry, 127
Bewick, Thomas, 88, 98
Bible type, 35
Biblioteca Laurenziana, 11
Bibliothèque Nationale, 11
Biemiller, Reynard, 101, 102
Biow, Margo, 137
Birnbaum, Abe, 102
Birrell, Augustine, 117
Blado type, 52

Blake, William, 70
Blake Collection of Mrs. Landon K. Thorne, The, 126
Blizard, Leonard, 17
Blumenthal, George, 107
Bodleian Library, 22
Bodoni, Giambattista, 30, 125, 127, 130
Bodoni type, 49, 52, 53, 125
Bollingen Foundation, 114
Bond, W. H., 118
Book in America: A History of the Making and Selling of Books in the United States, The (Lehmann-Haupt), 132
Book Club of California, 26–27
Book Collector's Packet, The, 45–46
Book Typography, 1815–1965, in Europe and the United States of America (Day, ed.), 132
Boston Museum of Fine Arts, 103
Boston Public Library, 75, 136, 140
Boston Society of Printers, 33
Boy's Will, A (Frost), 41
Bradley, Will, 26, 88, 93, 138
B. R. Marks & Remarks, 88
Bremer Presse, 14, 35, 36, 54, 55, 61, 64, 107
Breton, Nicholas, 89, 119
Brooks, Van Wyck, 113
Bühler, Curt F., 122
Bullen, Henry Lewis, 26, 76
Bulmer, William, 30, 130
Bulmer type, 51, 94, 120, 125, 131
Bunyan, John, 70
Burch, W. I., 56
Burtin, Will, 142

Calder, Alexander, 94–95
Calder, Louisa, 95
Caledonia type, 52, 139
Cambridge University Press, 43, 67
Candide (Voltaire), 21
Carnegie Institute of Technology, 26, 76
Caslon type, 13, 52, 134
Caxton, William, 122
Centaur type, 50, 52, 54, 64, 66, 107, 108, 137
Central European Manuscripts (Harrsen), 120

Cerf, Bennett, 20–21, 37, 38, 84, 85, 90
Chappell, Warren, 35, 93, 94, 102, 142
Chicago Society of Typographic Arts, 27
Childs, Bernard, 102
Chinese Calligraphy and Painting in the Collection of John M. Crawford, Jr., 121
Ching Ming Shang Ho, 109
Chiswick Press, 30
"Christmas Trees" (Frost), 41
Clapp, Frederick Mortimer, 113
Clarke, Bert, 142
Cleland, Thomas Maitland, 13–14, 26, 43, 93, 94, 117, 127, 138
Cloister Old Style type, 50
Cloisters, 107
Club of Odd Volumes, 120
Cobden-Sanderson bindings, 124
Cocteau, Jean, 110
Cohen, Herman, 128
Coleman, Carroll, 77, 142
Colish, Abe, 43, 127
Collected Poems of Robert Frost, 21, 38–40, 41, 46
Collins, Frances, 83
Colonial Printer, The (Wroth), 132
Colophon, The, 43–45, 119, 120
Columbia University Press, 28, 105
Compromise of the King of the Golden Isles (Lord Dunsany), 117
Conjugal Felicity, On, 88
Conkwright, P. J., 125, 142
Continental Type Founders Company, 15, 89
Cook, Howard, 42, 94
Cooper, Oswald, 32, 75
Cooper Union, 12
Coppard, A. E., 81
Cornell University, 8, 46, 140
Cranach Presse, 14, 36, 90
Crane, Hart, 83
Crawford, John M., Jr., 121
Crutchley, Brooke, 57
Culprit Fay and Other Poems (Drake), 117
Cummington Press, 77
Curry, John Steuart, 93
Curtis Paper Company, 101, 102
Curwen Press, 43

146

Dahlstrom, Grant, 27, 142
Dante type, 52
Dartmouth College Library, 132
Davidson, Marshall B., 108
Davy Crockett, American Comic Legend
  (Dorson, ed.), 91, 92
Day, Kenneth, 132
Day of Doom, The (Wigglesworth), 90
Daye, Matthew, 133
Daye, Stephen, 133
Dean, Mallette, 93
Decker, Blanche, 31
de Colines, Simon, 130
Deepdene type, 51
de Leon, Moses, 92
De Roos, S. H., 37
de Tournes, Jean, 129, 130
De Vinne, Theodore Low, 30, 88, 106,
  116, 135
Didot, Pierre, 30, 130
*Dolphin, The: A Journal of the Making
  of Books*, 46, 68
Donne, John, 9
Dorson, Richard M., 91
Doves Press, 10, 50, 121
Dowson, Ernest, 117
Draeger Frères, 108
Drake, Joseph Rodman, 117
Dreiser, Theodore, 9, 69
Dreyfus, John, 11, 57
Dumbarton Oaks, 25
Duncan, Harry A., 77, 142
Dürer, Albrecht, 96
Dwiggins, William Addison, 26, 45, 52,
  75, 88, 93, 94, 138–139, 142

Ecclesiastes (Spiral Press), 92, 96
Eckerstrom, Ralph E., 142
Eclogues of Virgil (Cranach Presse), 36
Eden Hill Press, 101
Edwards, Alfred C., 41
Eichenberg, Fritz, 42, 98–99
*Eighteenth-Century Studies in Honor of
  Donald F. Hyde* (Bond, ed.), 118
Eisenman, Alvin, 78, 79, 128, 142
Electra type, 52, 139
Eliot, John, 133
Elzevier Press, 122
Emerson, Ralph Waldo, 58

Emerson type, 53–59, 65, 66, 70, 83,
  92, 93, 96, 98, 100, 103, 107, 123
Emmett, Burton, 44
*English Drawings and Watercolors,
  1550–1850*, 126
English Monotype Corporation, 11, 50,
  52, 56, 58–59, 108
Enschedé Foundry, 37
Estienne, Robert, 130
Ettenburg, Eugene, 89
Eve type, 35, 89
Everson, William, 61
Eyre & Spottiswood, 58

Fairbanks, Thomas N., 14
Fairfield type, 52, 119, 139
Fantl, Ernestine, 83
Fass, John, 28, 29
Fathers and Sons (Turgenev), 99
Fell type, 9
Fern, Alan, 128
Fiene, Ernest, 89
Filene, Edward A., 111
Fine Print, 45
Fleuron, 46
Forgue, Norman, 46
Fortney, Frank, 28, 121
43 American Typographic Designers
  (Blumenthal, ptr.), 141
Forum type, 51
Four Gospels (Gill, des.), 11
Fournier, Pierre Simon, 30
Fournier type, 52
Fraktur type, 34
Franck, Peter, 62
Frankel, Walter, 122
Franklin, Benjamin, 134
Frasconi, Antonio, 42, 83, 97–98
Frick, Henry Clay, 113
Frick Collection, 25, 70, 113
Friedlander, Henri, 70
Frost, Leslie, 41
Frost, Robert, 21, 37, 38–42, 81, 99–100,
  105, 119, 120, 140
Fust & Schoeffer, 122, 130

Gág, Wanda, 90, 94
Gannett, Lewis, 91
Ganso, Emil, 94

Garamond, Claude, 51, 52
Garamond type, 51, 52, 90, 121
Garnett, Porter, 26, 76
Gates, John M., 109, 110
Gebrauchsgraphik, 46
Gehenna Press, 83, 101
General Theological Seminary, 25
Gentry, Helen, 43, 75
Gibbings, Robert, 11
Gill, Eric, 11, 36, 52, 61, 88, 110
Gilliss, Walter, 117
Giusti, George, 142
Glick, Milton, 28
Glover, Jose, 133
Goddard, William, 134
Godine, David R., 78, 126, 131, 136
Golden, William, 142
Golden Cockerel Press, 11
Golden type, 50
Goldin, Judah, 70
Goodhue, Bertram Grosvenor, 50, 93
Gordon, Ronald, 75
Goudy, Frederic W., 4, 13, 26, 32, 43, 45, 51, 52, 57, 75, 87, 88, 93, 117, 137–138
Goudy Modern type, 51
Goudy New Style type, 51
Goudy Old Style type, 51
Goudy Text type, 51
Grabhorn, Edwin and Robert, 27, 29, 89, 93, 142
Grabhorn Press, 21, 27, 43, 75, 93, 105
Gralla, Howard I., 79
Granite and Cypress (Jeffers), 61
Granniss, Ruth S., 44
Green, Charles R., 140
Green, John, 134
Green, Jonas, 134
Greene, Belle da Costa, 107, 118, 119, 120, 122
Gregynog Press, 11
Grier, Harry D. M., 113
Griffith, C. H., 52, 57, 139
Griffo, Francesco, 49, 50, 130
Grolier, Jean, 116–117
Grolier Club, 25, 44, 75, 84, 106, 116, 117, 118, 120, 139
Grolier Club, 1884–1967: An Informal History, The (Winterich), 116

Grolier 75, 102, 118
Grover, Sherwood, 75
Grushkin, Philip, 42, 101, 102, 110
Guinzburg, Harold K., 9
Gutenberg, Johann, 3, 29, 34, 48, 49, 61, 114, 128
Gutenberg Bible, 34, 49, 61, 114, 116, 130

Hadassah type, 70
Haddon Craftsmen, 85
Hadriano type, 51
Haight, Mrs. Sherman P., 122
Hamady, Walter, 78
Hammer, Caroline Reading, 78
Hammer, Victor, 59, 78, 93, 95, 142
Harbor Press, 28, 43, 75
Harcourt, Brace & World, 97, 98
Harrison, G. B., 70
Harrsen, Meta, 120
Hart, James D., 105
Harvard University Press, 43, 76, 111, 137
Hawthorn House, 28, 43, 75
Healy, George, 140
Heckscher, August, 112, 124
Heckscher, Charles, 75, 112
Hemingway, Ernest, 10
Hendrickson, James, 13, 28, 79
Henry Holt & Company, 17, 19, 37, 39, 41
Hildreth, E. L., & Company, 45
History of the Nonesuch Press (Dreyfus), 11
History of the Printed Book, A, 68
History of Printing in America, With a Biography of Printers and an Account of Newspapers, The (Thomas), 132
Hitchings, Sinclair, 78
Hoe, Robert, Jr., 116
Hoell, Louis, 54, 59
Hofer, Philip, 103, 109
Hoffman, George, 14, 15, 17, 18–19, 47
Holt, Rinehart & Winston, 41, 42, 100
Horne, Herbert, 50
Horton, Allen, 101
Houghton, Arthur A., Jr., 109, 110, 111
Houghton, Henry O., 135
Houghton, Mifflin & Company, 135

Howe, Walter L., 142
Hoyem, Andrew, 75
Hroswitha Club, 122
Hubbard, Elbert, 135, 139
Huebsch, B. W., 9, 124
Hugo, Harold, 121
Hunter, Dard, 26, 63–64, 139–140
Huntington Library, 129
Hurlburt, Allen F., 142
Hypnerotomachia Poliphili, 130

Imprimerie Royale, 130
Imprint, The, 46
Insel Verlag, 36
Institute of Paper Chemistry, 64
Intertype, 51
Italian Influence on American Literature
   (Barrett), 118
Italian Manuscripts (Harrsen), 120
Ivins, William M., 127, 128, 129

Jaffé, Aniela, 115
Jaffé, Arthur, 70, 121
Janson type, 52, 70
Jeffers, Robinson, 37, 61, 110
Jenson, Nicolaus, 30, 49, 50, 130
Jenson type, 53, 63
Joanna type, 11
Johnson, Henry Lewis, 45
Johnson, Herbert H., 80
Johnson, John, 57
Johnson, Marmaduke, 133
Johnson, Thomas H., 91
Johnston, Edward, 35, 36, 53
Johnston, Paul, 46
Jones, Howard Mumford, 90
Journal of the American Institute of
   Graphic Arts, 124
Joyce, James, 9, 10, 27
Jung, Carl Gustav, 114

Kacmarcik, Frank T., 142
Kelleher, Bradford D., 108
Kelmscott Press, 3, 4, 35, 50, 121
Kennedy, John F., 100–101, 113
Kennedy, Mrs. John F., 100
Kennerley type, 51
Kent, Henry Watson, 57, 106–108, 118
Kent, Rockwell, 21, 93

Kessler, Harry, 36
Keynes, Geoffrey, 70
Kibre, Pearl, 115
King Library Press, 79
Kittredge, William A., 27
Klingspor Type Foundry, 35, 37, 43
Klopfer, Donald, 20–21, 84, 85, 86
Knoedler Art Gallery, 19
Knopf, Alfred A., 25, 26, 79, 88, 92, 139
Koberger, Anton, 130
Koch, Rudolf, 34–35, 89, 99
Kramer, Sidney, 105
Kredel, Fritz, 35, 99, 108
Kroll, Leon, 110
Kup, Karl, 110

Laboratory Press, 76
LaGuardia, Fiorello H., 107
Lakeside Press, 27, 43, 139
Landeck, Armin, 42, 102
Lankes, J. J., 42, 102
Lanston Monotype Corporation, 52
Lask, Thomas, 136
Lathem, Edward Connery, 78, 127, 132,
   136
Laver, James, 71
Lawson, Alexander S., 80
Leaves of Grass (Whitman), 21
Lee, Marshall, 142
Lehmann-Haupt, Hellmut, 132
Leighton, Clare, 102
Lenox Collection, 133
Lerner, Abe, 89, 90
Leslie, Robert L., 88
Lewisohn, Adolph, 20
Liebaers, H., 141
Lime Kiln Press, 61
Limited Editions Club, 13, 25, 46, 61,
   66–68, 71, 81, 92, 93, 99, 102, 138
Lindenmeyr Paper Corporation, 75
Linotype, 5, 12, 23, 51, 52, 54, 60, 135
Lionni, Leo, 142
Liturgica type, 35
Liveright, Horace, 21
Lodging for the Night, A (Stevenson),
   117
Loos, Melvin, 28
Love and Joy About Letters (Shahn), 96
Love Poems (Donne), 9

149

Low, Joseph, 42, 93, 101, 142
Lubalin, Herb, 142
Luciani, John, 127
Lustig, Alvin, 142
Lutetia type, 37, 38, 52, 90
Lyrics of François Villon, The, 61, 62, 63, 65, 66

McCurdy, Michael, 103
McElderry, Margaret, 97
McGuire, William, 115
MacIver, Loren, 102
McMurtrie, Douglas C., 45
MacPhail, Ian, 115, 116
Macy, George, 13, 40, 46, 61, 63, 66, 67-70, 93, 99
Maillol, Aristide, 36, 90
Manhattanville College, 25, 114
Manso, Leo, 42
Manutius, Aldus. *See* Aldus Manutius
Marchbanks, Hal, 13, 14, 16, 17, 32
Marchbanks Press, 13, 19, 43, 45, 66, 104
Mardersteig, Giovanni, 52, 67, 141
Marks, Saul, 27, 29, 142
Marsh, Reginald, 27, 29, 69
Martin, Noel, 142
Martin, Stefan, 42, 92, 101
Mary Flagler Cary Music Collection, 125
Matisse, Henri, 27, 67, 93
Melbert B. Cary, Jr., Graphic Arts Collection, 59, 80
Melcher, Frederic G., 41, 42
Mellon, Mary Conover (Mrs. Paul), 114-116, 126
Mellon, Paul, 114-116, 126
Meredith, George, 3
Mergenthaler Linotype Company, 23, 51, 57, 86, 139
Meriden Gravure Company, 115, 116, 119, 121, 124, 131
Merker, K. K., 77
Merrymount Press, 4, 6, 20, 22, 137
Merrymount type, 50
Metropolitan Museum of Art, 20, 25, 81, 106-108, 109, 127
Meynell, Francis, 10, 11, 43, 67
Miers, Earl Schenck, 101
Miller, Edward Alonzo, 13

Milne, A. A., 100
minuscule, Carolingian, 49
Modern Library, 20, 21, 37
Modern Love (Meredith), 3
Monotype, 23, 51, 52. *See also* English Monotype Corporation
Montague Press, 138
Montaigne type, 50
Montallegro type, 50
Moore, Marianne, 110
Morgan, Alexander P., 122
Morgan, J. Pierpont, 118, 119
Morgan Library. *See* Pierpont Morgan Library
Morison, Stanley, 52, 56, 58, 88, 141
Morris, William, 3, 10, 35, 50, 68, 130
Morrow, Mrs. Dwight, 66
Moses, Robert, 107
Mosher, Thomas B., 3, 135
Multhauf, Robert, 115
Munder, Norman T. A., 32
Murdock, Kenneth B., 90
Museum of Modern Art, 25, 81, 82-83, 97, 103
My Life With Paper (Hunter), 140

Nash, John Henry, 27, 49, 50, 117, 139
Nash, Ray, 46, 78, 128
Nason, Thomas W., 41, 42, 76, 99, 120
Nast, Cyril, 32
National Arts Club, 13, 32
National Cathedral, 25
Nature (Emerson), 58, 62
Nelson, Robert W., 76
Neruda, Pablo, 37, 97
Nesheim, Kenneth, 129
Neumann, J. B., 15
New Colophon, The, 45
New School for Social Research, 74, 75, 99
New York Public Library, 74, 109, 110, 129, 133, 136
New York Times, 71, 131, 136
Newberry Library, 128, 140
Nitsche, Erik, 142
Noguchi, Isamu, 110
Nonesuch Century, The, 11
Nonesuch Press, 9, 10, 11, 21

Odyssey of Homer (Rogers, des.), 65
O'Hagan, Jim, 127
Oldenburg, Peter, 108, 111, 142
Olin Library, 140
Oliphant Press, 75
Oswald, John Clyde, 32, 132
Overbrook Press, 93, 138
Oxford Lectern Bible, 73, 87
Oxford University Press, 9, 11, 37, 43, 57, 67, 73, 137

Pantheon Books, 25, 92, 94
Parker, James, 133
Parks, William, 134
Peckham, John, 121
Peignot, Charles, 52
Pen Print Bold type, 16
Penmaen Press, 103
Perishable Press Limited, 78
Perpetua type, 11, 28, 52, 131
Peter Pauper Press, 28, 75, 89, 93
Peter Piper's Practical Principles of Plain and Perfect Pronunciation, 99
Petrocelli, Frank, 127
Phillida and Coridon (Breton), 89, 119
Philobiblon, 46
Picasso, Pablo, 27, 67, 93
Pickering, William, 30, 130
Pierpont Morgan Library, 25, 26, 43, 44, 86, 107, 118–131, 140, 141
Pierrot of the Minute (Dowson), 117
Pierson College Press, 79, 126
Pilgrim's Progress (Bunyan), 70
Plantin, Christopher, 30, 130
Plantin Press, 29, 43, 133
Poe, Edgar Allan, 90
Poems of Edgar Allan Poe, 90
Poeschl & Trepte, 36
Poetical Works of Edward Taylor, The, 91
Poetry Society of America, 110
Poliphilus type, 52, 70
Porter, Priscilla Manning, 122
Prairie Press, 77
Press of A. Colish, 127
Primer type, 52, 139
Primitives (Weber), 16, 17, 73, 89
Princeton University Press, 19, 92
Print, 46

Printed Book in America, The (Blumenthal), 4, 71, 92, 132, 136
Printers' Marks in the Pierpont Morgan Library (Adams), 122
Printing in the Americas (Oswald), 132
Printing Art, The, 45
Printing and Graphic Arts (PaGA), 46
Printing with the Handpress (Allen), 65
Printing Types: Their History, Forms, and Use (Updike), 76, 137
Proffitt, Charles, 105
Publishers Weekly, 41
Pynson, Richard, 122
Pynson Printers, 19, 21, 28, 43, 44, 48, 93, 116, 119, 120, 122

Quarto-millenary, A, 67
Quattrocentisteria (Hewlett), 117

Rand, Paul, 142
Random House, 10, 20, 21, 25, 26, 37, 81, 84, 85, 90
Rascoe, Burton, 69
Ratdolt, Erhard, 122
Ray, Gordon N., 119
Reading, W. Gay, 79
Recalling Peter: The Life and Times of Peter Beilenson and His Peter Pauper Press, 88
Reed, Philip, 142
Reedijk, C., 141
Reichl, Ernst, 10
Renner, Paul, 34
Resurrection (Tolstoy), 99
Review of Acquisitions, 1949–1968, A, 125
Richardson, Norman, 127
Ritchie, Ward, 27, 43, 142
Riverside Press, 11, 50, 135, 137
Robinson, Boardman, 102
Rochester Institute of Technology, 59, 80, 108
Rockefeller, John D., Jr., 107
Rockefeller University Press, 102
Rockland Editions, 81, 90–91
Rogers, Bruce, 4, 9, 11, 13, 20, 26, 27, 30, 32, 43, 50, 54, 57, 62, 63, 65, 67, 71, 73, 79, 87, 88, 93, 106, 113, 117, 118, 122, 125, 127, 130, 135, 137

151

Rollins, Carl Purington, 26, 79, 88,
    106, 117, 138, 142
Romanée type, 37
Roosevelt, Franklin D., 66, 81; collected
    papers and addresses of, 84–86, 123
Rose and the Ring, The (Thackeray), 119
Rosenbach, A. S. W., 26
Rosenbach, Juan, 122
Rosenman, Samuel I., 84–86
R. R. Donnelley, 27
Rudge, William Edwin, printing house
    of, 6, 12, 13, 20, 30, 32, 75, 79, 93,
    137, 139
Russell, J., 134
Russell-Rutter Company, 28, 121
Ruzicka, Rudolph, 26, 52, 93, 139
Ryskamp, Charles, 124, 125, 128, 130

Salter, George, 101, 112, 142
Samuel, Maurice, 92
Saturday Review of Literature, 21
Schlosser, Leonard, 75
Schoeffer, Peter, 122, 130
Schoolmaster Printer of St. Alban's, 122
Scotch Roman type, 52, 94
Scotus, Octavianus, 122
Secret, The (Milne), 100
Sefer Ha-Zohar (Book of Splendor), 92
Shahn, Ben, 70, 71, 74, 92, 95–96
Shahnameh ("Book of Kings"), 111
Shaw, George Bernard, 27
Shenker, Israel, 131
Sickman, Laurence, 121
Signature, 46
Silver, Rollo, 132
Simon, Howard, 61
Simon & Schuster, 26
Simons, Anna, 35
Sister Carrie (Dreiser), 69
Sistina type, 121
Smith, Rae, 127
Sonnenberg, Benjamin, 125
Soshensky, David, 93, 101
Southworth Press, 45
Spectrum type, 37
Spinach From Many Gardens, 87
Spiral Press Through Four Decades, The,
    122, 123
Spoon River Anthology (Masters), 103

Spratling, William, 66
Stamperia del Santuccio, 78
Stanford, Alfred, 44
Steeple Bush (Frost), 102
Stein, Gertrude, 10
Stein, Max, 69
Steuben Glass, 109–111
Stevenson, Robert Louis, 117
Stinehour, Roderick, 78, 126, 136
Stinehour Press, 46, 115, 116, 126, 131
Stone, William, 142
Stone Wall Press, 77
Sutnar, Ladislav, 142

Taft School, 122
Talmud, 70, 92
Taylor, Edward, 91
Thackeray, William Makepeace, 119
Thistle Press, 122
Thomas, Isaiah, 132, 134
Thompson, Bradbury, 142
Thompson, Edmund B., 28
Three Essays (Birrell), 117
Times Literary Supplement, 123, 131, 136
Times New Roman type, 52
To Russia With Frost (Adams), 120
Tory, Geoffroy, 129, 130
Trafton, Howard, 76, 100
Troy type, 50
Twentieth Century Fund, 25, 111–112
Twenty-one Classic Typefaces for Book and
    Periodical Setting on Monotype
    Composing Machines, 59
Typographic Laboratory, 77
Typography, 46
Typophiles, 86–89, 97, 120
Typophiles Left to Their Own Devices,
    The, 87

Ulysses (Joyce), 10
University of Chicago Press, 133
Updike, Daniel Berkeley, 4, 6, 9, 22,
    26, 27, 30, 32, 33, 43, 50, 76, 93,
    106, 114, 122, 135, 137

Van Doren, Mark, 110
van Krimpen, Jan, 37, 38, 52, 88
Vassar College, 25, 114
Vatican Library, 11

Vérard, Antoine, 122
Viking Press, 9, 25, 26, 28
Villon, François. *See Lyrics of François Villon*
Vostre, Simon, 122
Voyages, Six Poems (Crane), 83

Walker, Emery, 36
Walker, Gay, 79
Walkowitz, Abraham, 20
Walpole Printing Office, 43, 89
Warde, Frederic, 52, 93, 107, 139
Waugh, Sidney, 109, 110
Wayside Press, 138
Weber, Max, 15, 16, 73
Weiss, E. R., 34, 67
Wells, James M., 128, 132
Wells College Press, 78
Wescott, Glenway, 83
Weyhe, E., 20, 92, 97
What I Am Pleased to Call My Education (Kent), 106, 118
Wheat, Carl, 105
Wheeler, Monroe, 83, 103
Whitman, Walt, 21, 98
Whittingham, Charles, 30
Wiebking, Robert, 54
Wiegand, Willy, 35–36, 64
Wigglesworth, Michael, 90
Wilbur, Richard, 94
William Rockhill Nelson Gallery of

Art, 121
Williams, William Carlos, 37, 110
Wilson, Woodrow, 8, 35
Windhover Press, 77
Winship, George Parker, 26, 27, 76
Winterich, John T., 44, 45, 105, 116, 118
Witten, II, Laurence C., 115
Wolff, Kurt, 36, 92, 94
Wong, Jeanyee, 101
Wood, Grant, 67, 93
Wood, Roland, 28
Woodcuts by Antonio Frasconi, 88, 97
Woolsey, John Munro, 10
World War I, 8, 27
World War II, 103–105, 106
Worthy Paper Company, 28, 65
Writing & Illuminating, & Lettering (Johnston), 53
Wroth, Lawrence C., 88, 120, 132

Yale University Library, 22, 79, 114
Yale University Press, 22, 43, 138
Yarmolinsky, Avrahm, 67
You Come Too (Frost), 41, 99

Zachrisson, Bror, 141
Zanders mill, 36
Zapf, Hermann, 52, 80, 88
Zeitlin, Jake, 26

Letterpress composition and printing in Baskerville and Bulmer types,

and binding, by the

STINEHOUR PRESS · LUNENBURG · VERMONT

Plates made and printed by the

MERIDEN GRAVURE COMPANY · MERIDEN · CONNECTICUT

*

TYPOGRAPHY BY JOSEPH BLUMENTHAL